Aircraft Systems

Conforti, Facundo
/ Facundo Conforti. - 1a ed. - Mar del Plata : Facundo Jorge Conforti, 2022.
150 p. ; 21 x 15 cm.

1. Escritura. I. TÌtulo.
CDD 808.027

Introduction

Aircraft Systems have been an under explored subject in flight academies. The truth is, a pilot must be familiar with each of their aircraft's systems before commencing their initial flights.

In this work, you will learn everything about the basic systems of the main light or small aircraft: landing gear, tires, flight controls, fuel, electricity, cables and control rods, control surfaces, and all the key systems that make up your aircraft's equipment.

Learning aircraft systems should take place during the initial flight hours for aviation students. This will provide them with the necessary tools to understand what is happening with the operation of each of these systems at all times. A particular skill that will maximize safety in flight operations.

All of us, as human beings, need to understand how our body functions to identify deficiencies and stay healthy. As pilots, we need to understand how our aircraft systems work to identify malfunctions and manage emergencies efficiently and safely.

Capt. Facundo Conforti

Biblioteca
Aeronáutica
aviación en simples pasos

Main

Chapter 1 – Structures

Chapter 2 – Landing gear

Chapter 3 – Propellers

Chapter 4 – Engines

Chapter 5 – Fuel

Chapter 6 – Flight instruments

Chapter 1

Structures

Biblioteca
Aeronáutica
aviación en simples pasos

Introduction

The aircraft structure includes the main structural elements of the aircraft that support the loads to which the aircraft is subjected in the air and on the ground. The primary components are the fuselage, wings, tail assembly, and flight controls.

Fuselage

The fuselage is the main structure or body of the aircraft. It carries passengers and crew in safe and comfortable conditions. The fuselage also provides space for controls, accessories, and other equipment. It transfers loads to and from the main wings, tail, fins, landing gear, and, in certain configurations, the engines. There are three main types of fuselage construction. First is the frame or truss type, which is generally used for light, non-pressurized aircraft.

Then there is the monocoque construction, which was primarily used in the early 20th century. Finally, there is the semi-monocoque fuselage, which is used in most non-pressurized aircraft.

Frame or Truss Fuselage: When a frame structure is used for the fuselage, the frame consists of lightweight steel tubes with minimal wall thickness, joined to form a triangular space frame. This creates the most rigid geometric shapes. Each tube carries a specific load, the magnitude of which depends on whether the aircraft is in the air or on the ground. This type of construction is strong, easy to build, and provides a relatively trouble-free basic layout.

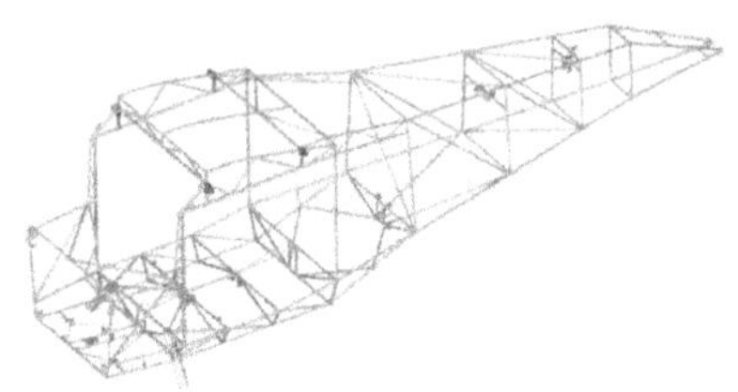

The frame is typically covered with a lightweight aluminum alloy or fabric skin to form a closed and aerodynamically efficient cargo transport compartment. The most characteristic example of this type of fuselage is the classic PIPER aircraft, model PA-11

Monocoque Fuselage: Monocoque is a French word meaning "single shell." In a monocoque structure, all loads are absorbed by a stressed skin, with only lightweight frames or internal formers to give the required shape. Due to its structural characteristics, even slight damage to the surface can seriously weaken the structure. To be a true monocoque, the structure would have no openings at all, like an ostrich egg; however, for practical purposes in an aircraft, openings must be provided for access and maintenance.

These openings must be reinforced to maintain the integrity of the structure. But once the aircraft doors are closed and all hatches and access panels are installed, the fuselage is, for all intents and purposes, a monocoque structure. Two aircraft built according to the monocoque principle were the plywood construction Roland CII (1915) and the Ford Trimotor (1926).

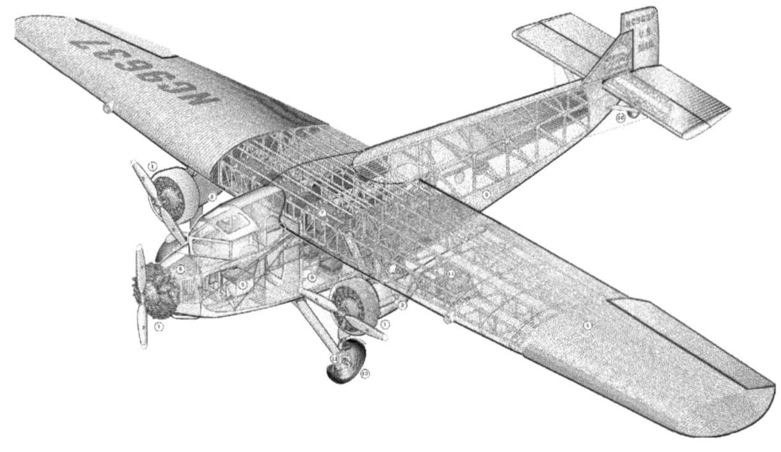

Semi-Monocoque Fuselage: As aircraft grew larger and air loads increased, it was found that pure monocoque structure was not strong enough. Additional structural members known as longerons were added to run along the length of the fuselage, connecting the frames. A lightweight alloy skin was then attached to the frames and longerons through riveting or adhesive bonding. This type of fuselage construction is called semi-monocoque.

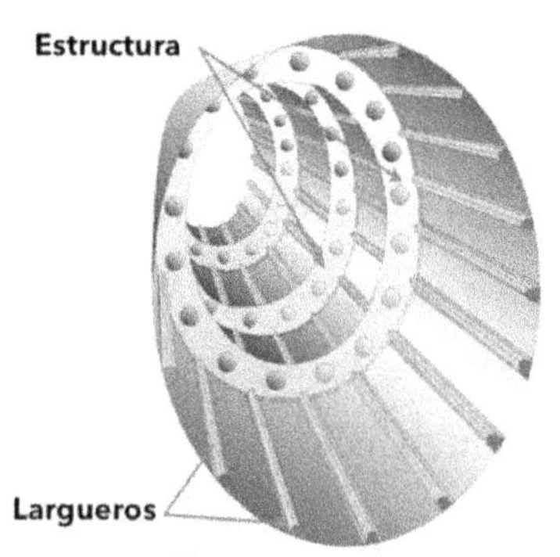

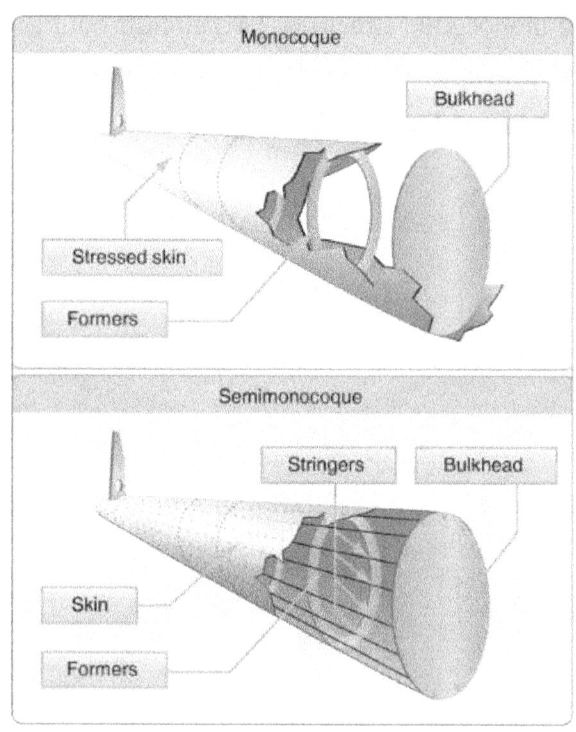

In semi-monocoque fuselages, the longerons and frames stiffen the skin (surface or wall), and the flight loads are shared between the skin and the structure beneath. Bulkheads are placed to separate different sections of the fuselage; for example, between the engine compartment and the passenger compartment.

The bulkhead has the same basic shape as the frames or formers but isolates one compartment almost completely from another. However, holes must be made in the bulkhead to allow control fittings, pipes, and electrical cables to pass through the length of the fuselage. Bulkheads are usually constructed much more substantially than the frames because they are subjected to greater loads. Additionally, the bulkhead separating the engine from the passenger compartment serves to delay the passage of fire from the engine to the rear in the event of a fire.

The choice of fuselage type responds to the aircraft's purpose and is determined by the manufacturer. The fuselage is considered the skeleton of the aircraft and must be correctly selected based on the class of flight intended for each aircraft.

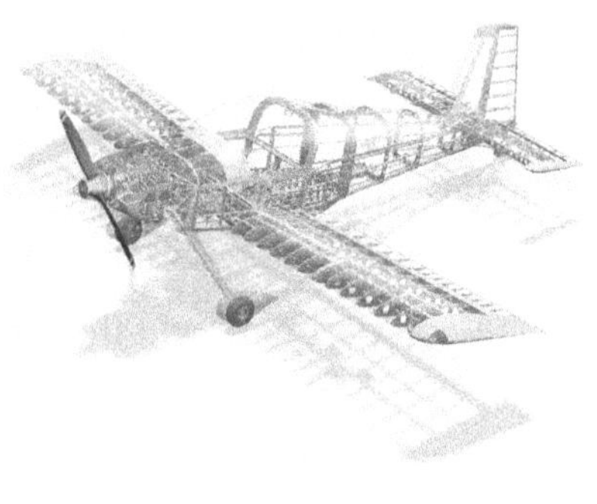

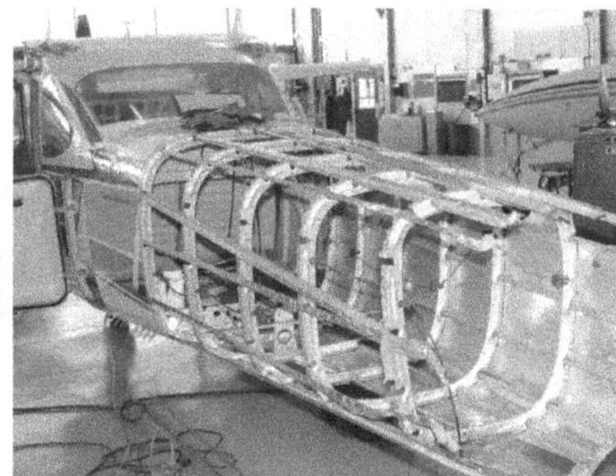

Wings

The wings of the main aircraft generate lift and, in level flight, support the weight of the aircraft in the air. When the aircraft is maneuvering, the wings will have to withstand loads that are several times the weight of the aircraft. Therefore, the wings must have sufficient strength and rigidity to do so. The degree of strength and rigidity is determined by the thickness of the wing. The thickness and type of construction used depend on the speed requirements of the aircraft.

Let's start with the most important aerodynamic structure of the aircraft: the wings. Most of the aerodynamic forces acting during flight are directed at them, and they are responsible for the aerodynamic effect that allows the aircraft to move through the air. As mentioned in previous sections, the wings are composed of a series of airfoil sections positioned next to each other along the entire wing surface.

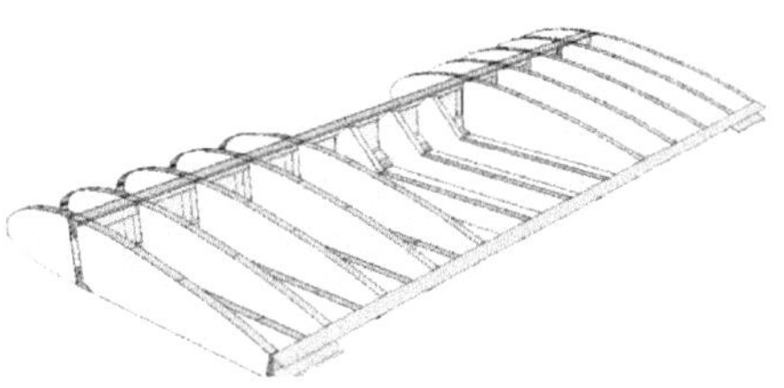

The number of airfoils will define the total wing area and its length, known as "wingspan" (the distance between the two wingtips). It is important to note that a greater wingspan results in a larger wing area, which in turn increases lift capacity compared to a shorter wingspan.

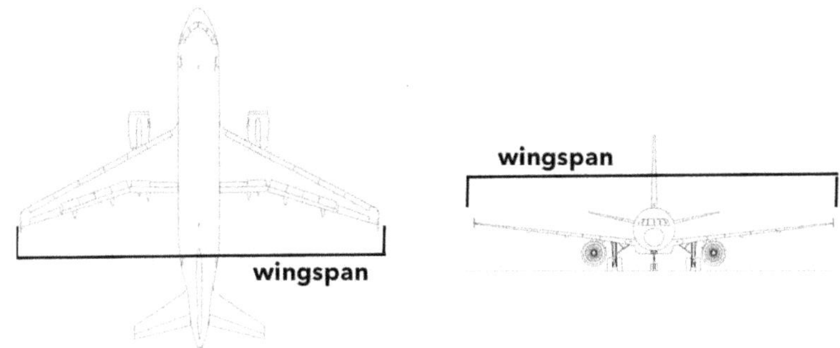

The load-bearing capacity of a wing is achieved by constructing it around one or more primary load-bearing members, which are designed to absorb bending stresses downward when on the ground and upward, backward, and torsional stresses during flight.

The main structural components of the wing are generally made from aluminum alloys, with composite materials such as fiberglass-reinforced plastic, carbon-reinforced plastic, and honeycomb structures used for fairings, control surfaces, and flaps, etc.

Bending stress relief is aided by placing the main fuel tanks within the wing. Wings can be constructed as single-skin, double-skin, or multi-skin. A conventional structure of the main wing would consist of front and rear spars, with a metal skin bonded to the spars to form a torsion box, countering the twisting forces.

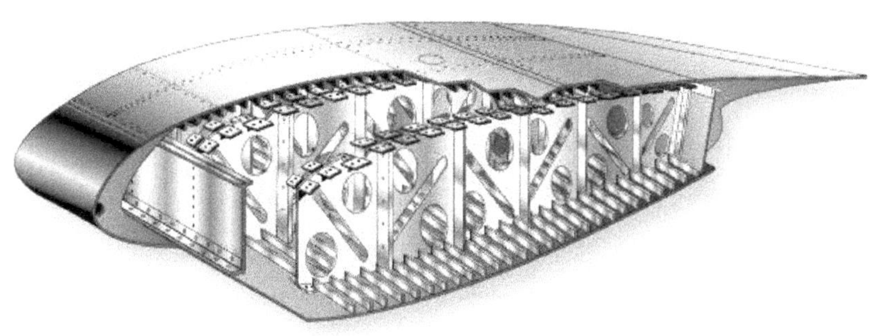

The skin of a wing helps support loads. It generates direct stresses in a spanwise direction in response to bending moments and also resists torsion. Struts are spanwise members that give rigidity to the wing by stiffening the skin in compression. Ribs maintain the aerodynamic shape of the wings, support the spars, and skin against bending, and transfer concentrated loads from the engines, landing gear, and control surfaces to the skin and spars.

The manufacturer of each aircraft defines the wingspan of the aircraft based on its intended purpose and also decides what type of wings to produce for the model. Wings can be classified according to the following variables:

- Position relative to the aircraft fuselage.
- Number of wings or planes on the same aircraft.
- Angle or "dihedral" of the wings.
- Specific shape of each wing.

The first classification is based on the position of the wings:

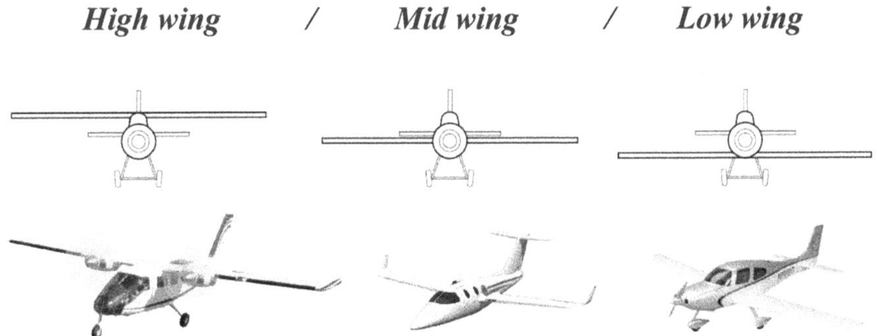

Each of these classifications refers to the position of the wings relative to the fuselage of the aircraft.

In addition, wings can have more than one plane in their structure, being:

Monoplane / Biplane / Triplane / Multiplane

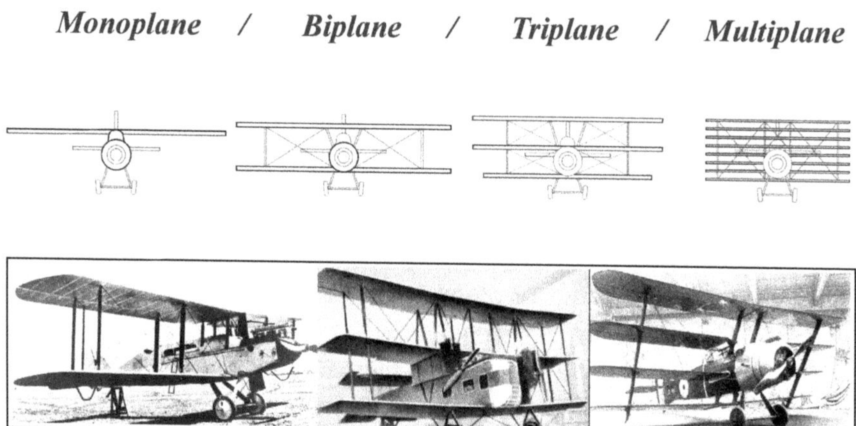

Another classification is based on the "sweep" angle of each wing design, which is the angle formed by the wing and the aircraft's transverse axis. Let's explore this further:

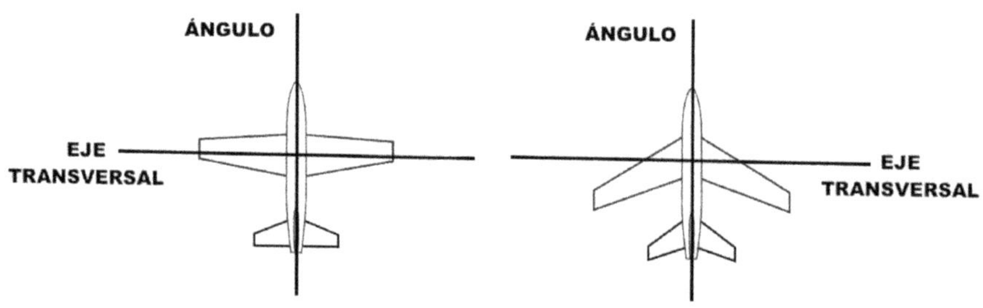

While this angle is usually a fixed value, there are designs with variable angles, typically assigned to combat aircraft.

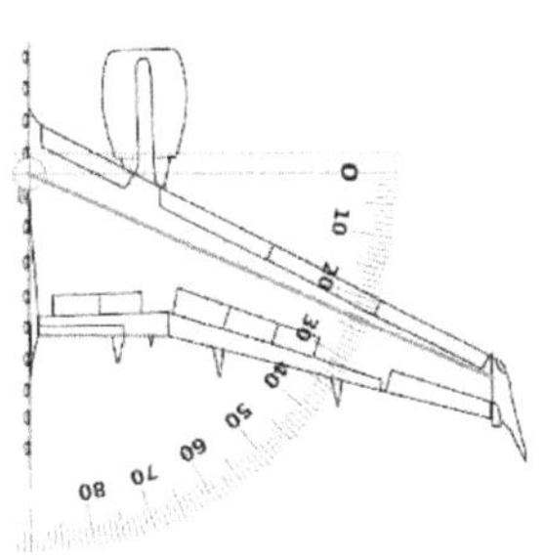

Straight wing

Swep-back wing

Variable geometry wing

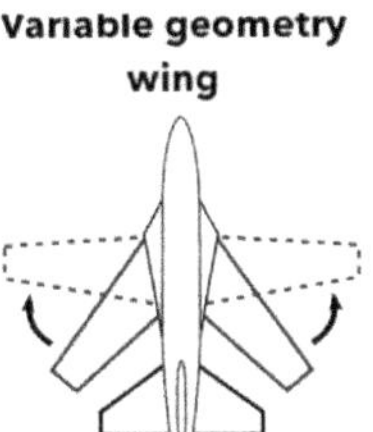

Another common variable in wing manufacturing is the "dihedral" angle, or the angle formed by the wing surface and the real horizon line.

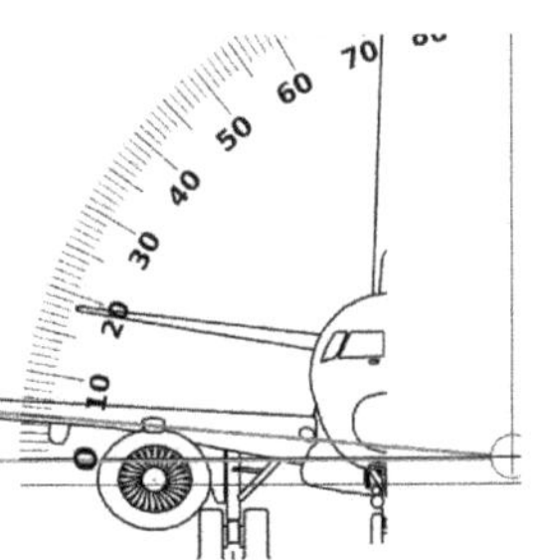

Dihedral positive

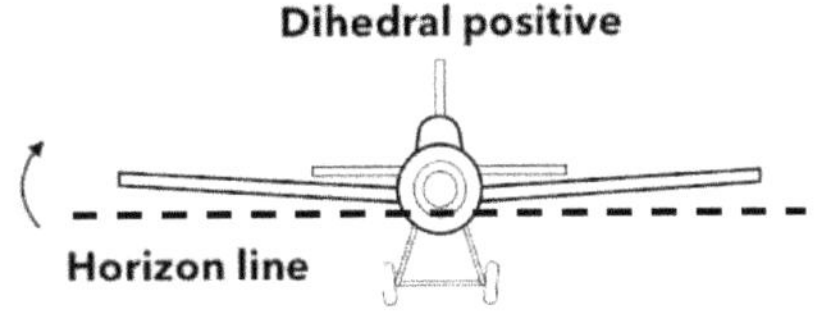

Dihedral negative

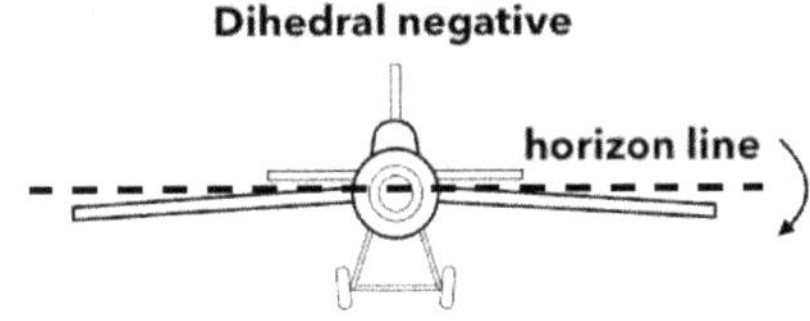

Dihedral positive

Dihedral negative

Lastly, the specific shape of the wing is also determined by the manufacturer. Based on the intended flight purposes of the aircraft, the manufacturer can opt for one of the following wing designs:

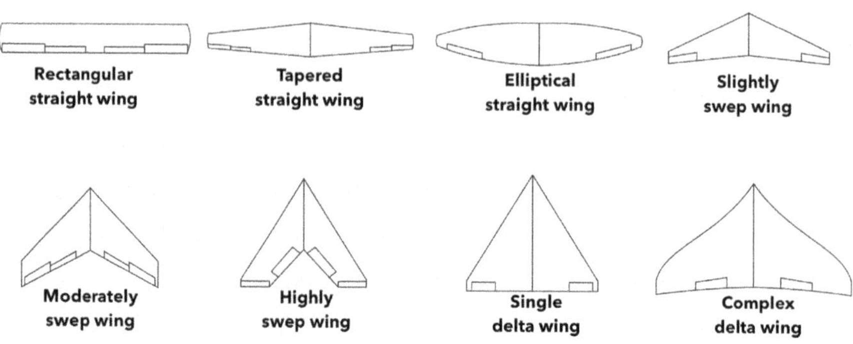

Wing Tips: Just as there are various wing designs, each can feature different designs for its tips, known as “wing tips” or “wing marginal edges.”

As described in the chapter on drag, the different designs of wing tips serve to reduce induced drag, among other factors. Similar to wing design, the shape of the wing tips is determined by the manufacturer.

Rounded Tip: A simple design that allows the air to flow from the lower surface (intradós) to the upper surface (extradós).

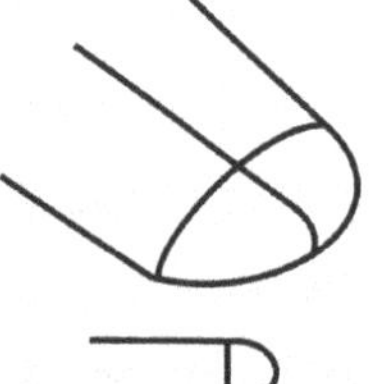

Tapered Edge: Unlike the previous one, at this edge the air does not flow easily from the lower to the upper surfaces, generating less induced resistance, so it is considered a more effective edge.

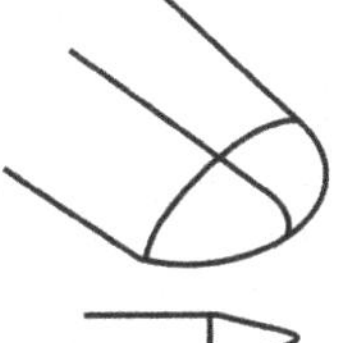

Straight Edge: Manufacturing edge simpler than the previous ones. It is based on a straight-shaped cross-section of the wing. The airflow passes from the lower to the upper surfaces easily and forms whirlwinds of more intense wing tips, but has a higher aerodynamic performance.

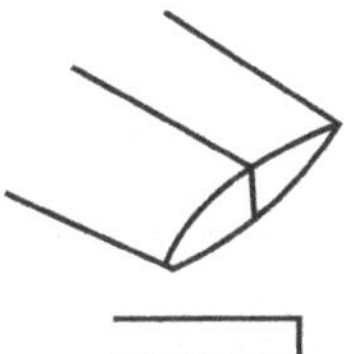

Hoerner Edge: Although it is a complex manufacturing edge, it provides one of the most efficient aerodynamic yields. It is formed with the straight upper surface to the end of the wing tip and the lower surface with a curvature of 30° at the final end of the wing

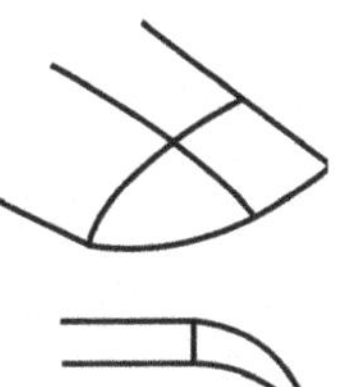

Concave Edge: Similar to the previous one but with its downward curvature, generating an extension of the wing surface and increasing its aerodynamic performance.

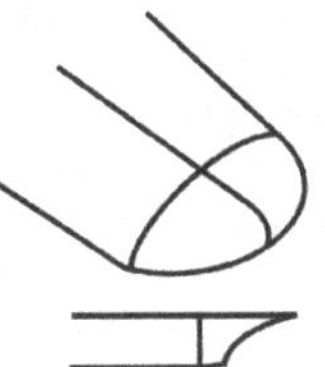

Convex Edge: Edge with induced resistance reduction benefits. The air that flows through the lower surface finds a barrier to ride on the upper surface and reduces the formation of whirlwinds of wingtips.

Rear Arrow Edge Complex manufacturing edge that delays the whirlwind formation section and reduces its intensity. Edge associated with high-speed aerodynamic profiles.

Plate Edge: An edge with induced resistance reduction but with an increase in parasitic resistance due to its shape and surface of direct impact with the air. An underused edge due to its complex manufacture and reduced benefits.

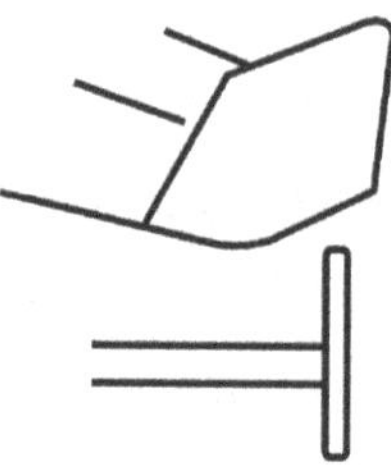

Winglets Edge: Edge considered as an induced resistance reducer. It prevents the passage of the flow of air coming from the lower surface and tries to reach the upper surface to form whirlwinds.

Front Arrow Edge: Edge associated with profiles in supersonic planes. It reduces twisting efforts and provides a lighter wing

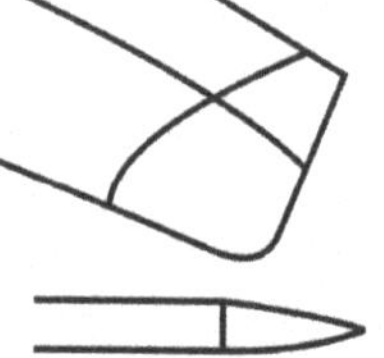

Control surfaces

Control surfaces are divided into two groups: primary control surfaces and secondary control surfaces. In the first group, the primary control surfaces include the ailerons, and the control surfaces on the tail section, namely the rudder and elevator. In the second group, the secondary control surfaces include other devices such as flaps, slats, and spoilers.

Ailerons

Considered as primary control surfaces, the ailerons are located at the rear edge of each wingtip. Their operation causes the aircraft to roll about its longitudinal axis.

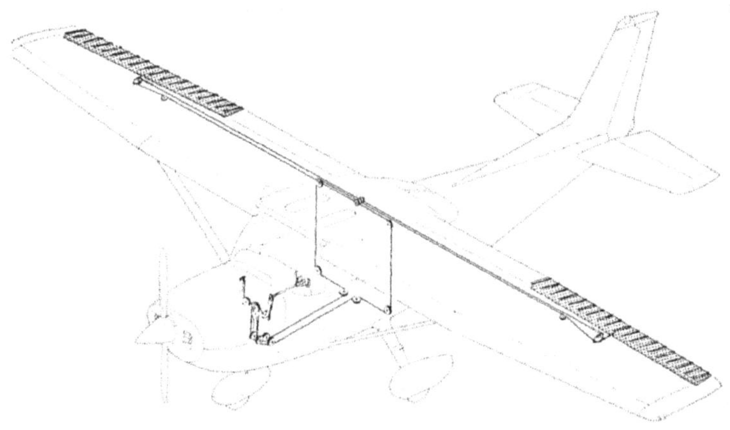

Their position at the wingtip is due to the fact that the aerodynamic effect exerted on the wing surface is greater in this area. Ailerons move asymmetrically. When the control yoke is turned to one side, the aileron on that wing rises, while the aileron on the opposite wing lowers, both deflecting at an angle proportional to the yoke's movement.

Taking a closer look at the entire flight control system, in the cockpit, two control columns are mechanically linked to a system of pulleys and cables that allow the movement not only of the ailerons but also of the elevator.

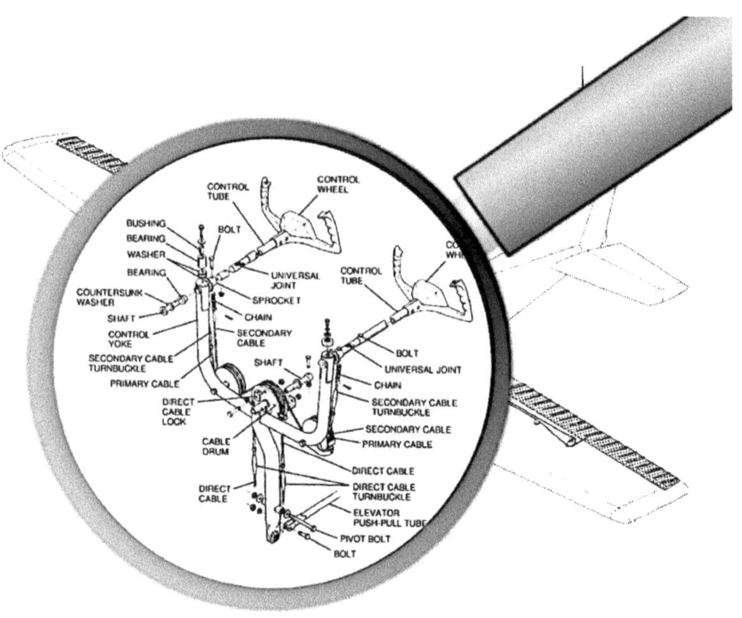

When the aileron on the wing, towards which the control column is moved, goes up, it reduces the curvature of that part of the wing, thereby reducing lift, which causes that wing to drop. Conversely, the aileron on the opposite wing lowers, increasing the curvature and lift, causing that wing to rise. This combination of opposing effects produces the rolling motion.

For example, if you want to perform a right turn, one of the required actions will be to turn the control column to the right; the aileron on the right wing will rise, and with less lift, that wing will descend. On the contrary, the aileron on the left wing will lower, causing greater lift on that wing, which will ascend.

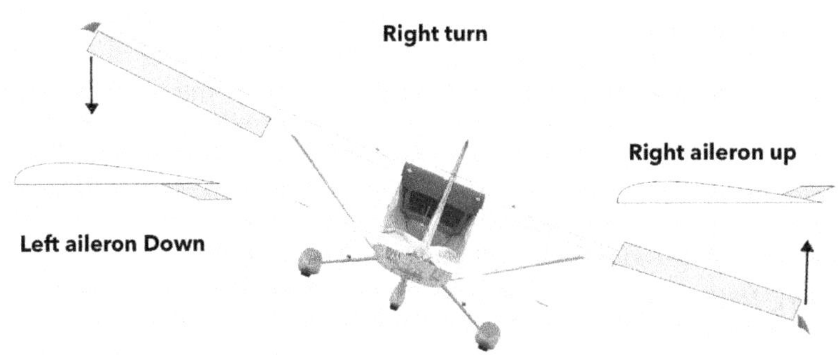

The following image represents the airfoil of the left wing, which gains curvature compared to the airfoil of the right wing, where the raised aileron reduces its curvature.

The greater the deflection of the control column towards one side, the greater the deflection of the ailerons, and the greater the difference in the curvature of the airfoil. As a result, the greater the difference in lift between the wings, the steeper the bank angle of the turn.

Stabilizer

Like ailerons, the parts that make up the stabilizer set are considered primary flight control surfaces. The empennage set is composed of two fixed structures and two moving structures that guarantee stability in flight.

Perpendicular to the position of the ailerons we find the vertical stabilizer (fixed surface) and next to it, the steering rudder (movable surface). Parallel to the position of the ailerons and perpendicular to the vertical stabilizer, we find the horizontal stabilizer rudder (fixed surface) that joins the depth rudder (moving surface). Let's see:

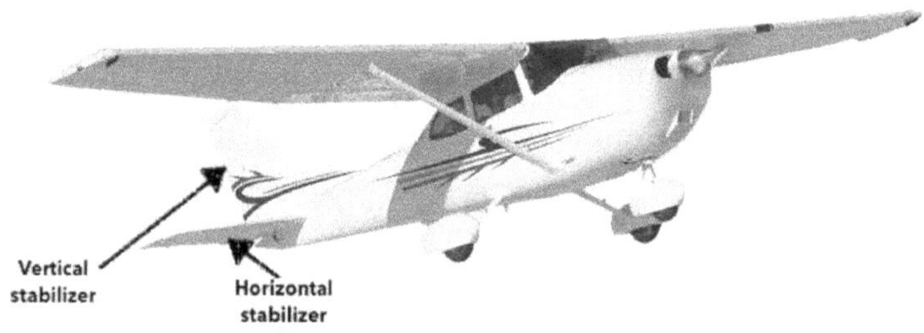

Similar to wings, stabilizers can vary their shape depending on the operating criterion that each manufacturer gives to their aircraft. We can divide the manufacture of the empennage into two large groups.

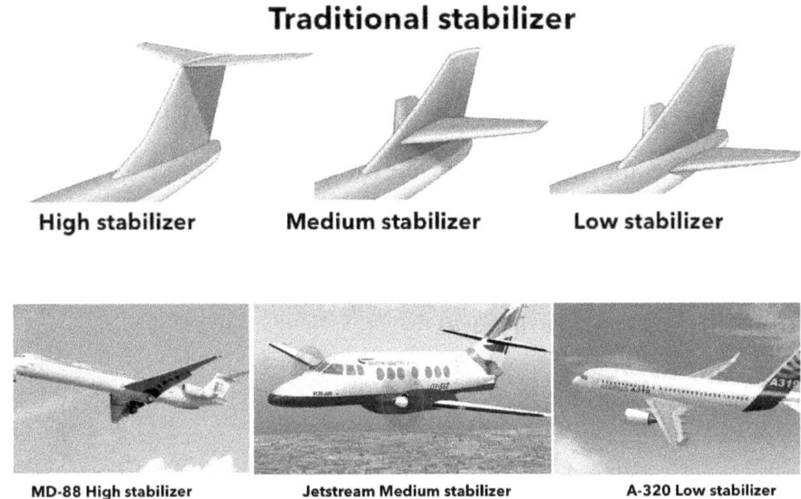

The other less popular or least used designs are special stabilizers and can be "V" stabilizers or "H" stabilizers, receiving their name depending on their shape. Let's see:

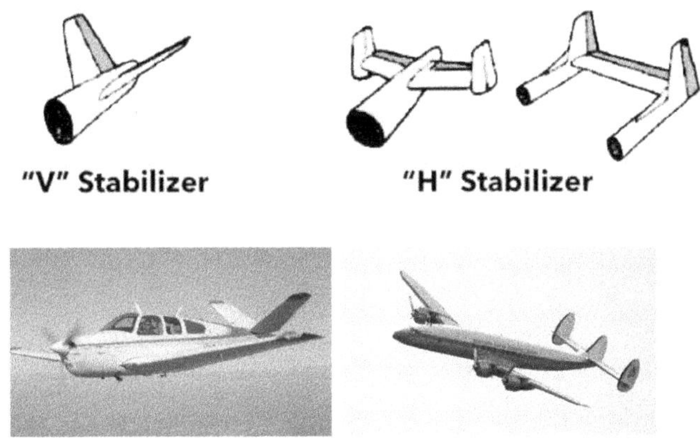

Considering that the stabilizers are operated manually by the pilot from the cockpit, their effectiveness is directly related to the force that the pilot exerts on the corresponding commands at the time of executing an action.

Horizontal Stabilizer

The movable section of the horizontal stabilizer is called the elevator. Like the ailerons, the elevator is connected to the control columns via cables and pulleys. However, unlike the ailerons, this control system moves in the same direction and simultaneously, either up or down, giving the aircraft pitch movement. It has one cable and pulley system for upward movement and another for downward movement.

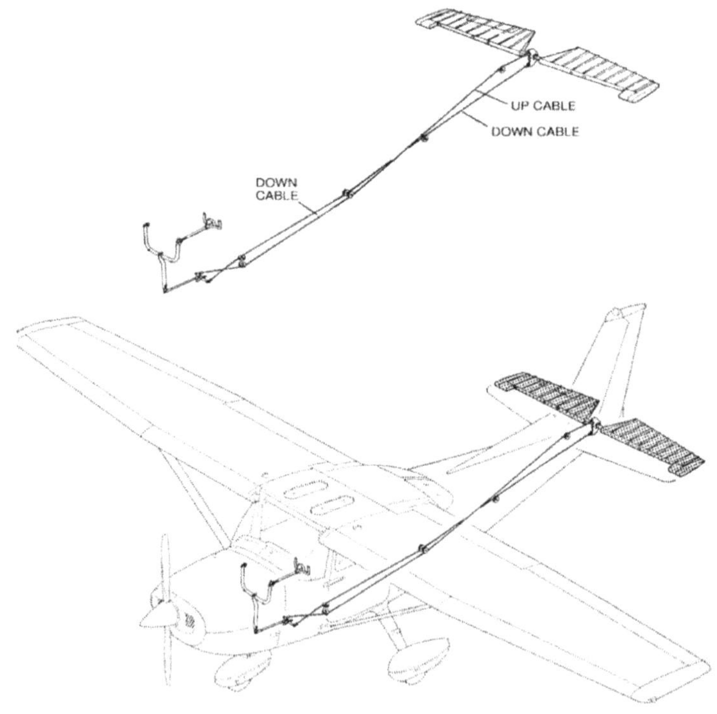

Associated with the elevator system, there is a compensation system known as TRIM installed. It is a wiring device that is attached to a flat surface located in the elevator that helps compensate up or down for the movement of this flight control. It is operated from the cockpit by means of a wheel located under the main panel.

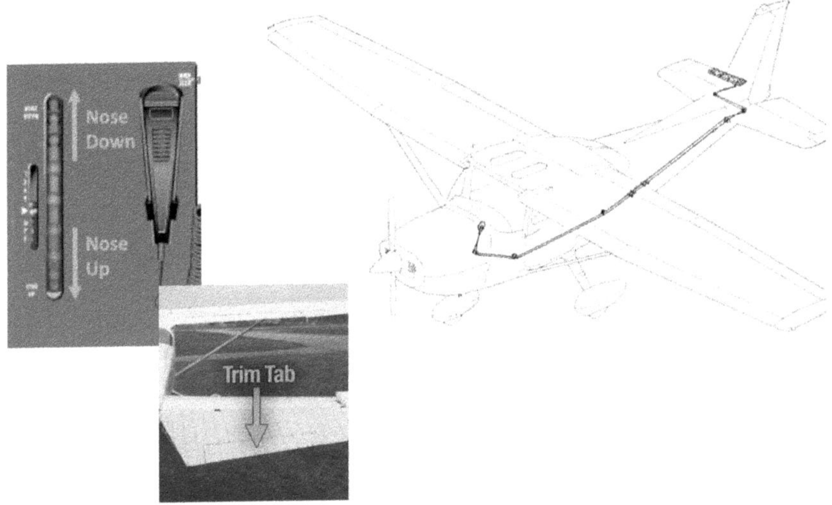

It is important to mention that these control surfaces are universal for all aircraft and respond to the same aerodynamic principle. The following image represents the same surfaces on an Airbus A320.

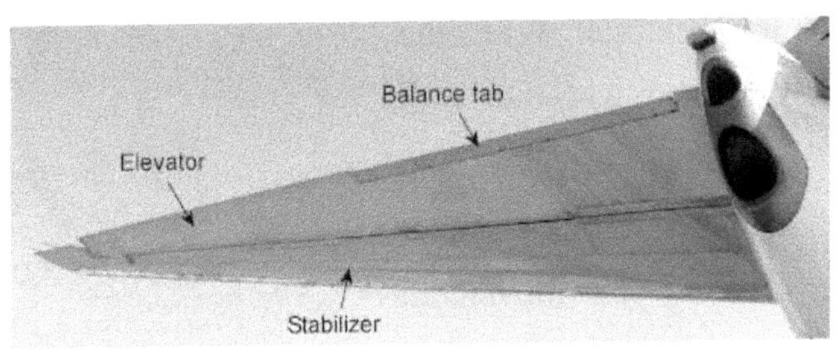

Estabilizador vertical

The movable section of the vertical stabilizer is called the rudder. The rudder system operates similarly to the previously mentioned systems. It is controlled from the cockpit through a system of pedals, which are mechanically linked with cables and pulleys to the control surface located on the vertical stabilizer.

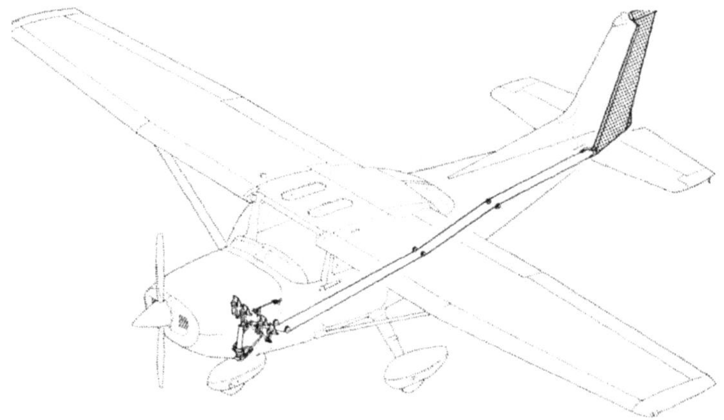

Inside the cockpit, beneath the main panel, there are two sets of pedals, one for each pilot. When the pilot applies pressure with their foot on one of the pedals, the cable and pulley mechanism moves the rudder surface to produce yaw movement for the aircraft.

In an A320, the operating principle is identical. Below the main panel, the pedals used to control the rudder are located.

Just like the elevator system, the rudder also has a trim system; however, this is an optional feature and is not installed in all aircraft models. Its function is identical to the elevator trim and is operated from the cockpit by a wheel or knob, depending on the model, which is moved left or right as needed. This control is located just below the elevator trim wheel.

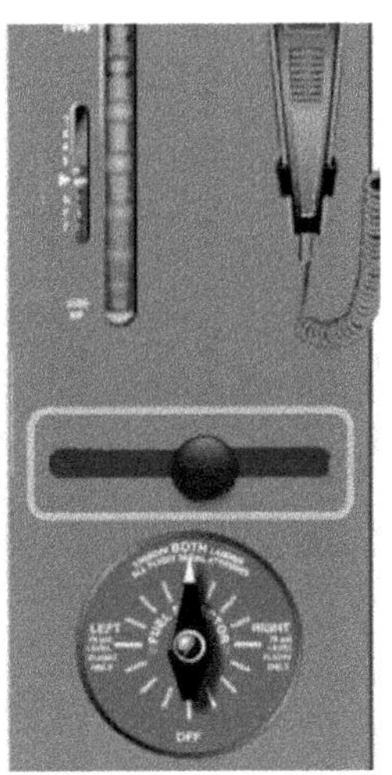

The second group of control surfaces are the secondary control surfaces: flaps, slats, and spoilers. In light aircraft, these control surfaces do not exist (e.g., Piper PA-11).

Flaps and Slats

FLAPS and SLATS are considered secondary flight controls. Located along the leading edge and the leaking edge, they are considered hight lift devices, that is, these devices can maximize the lift that a wing surface can produce in a certain flight situation.

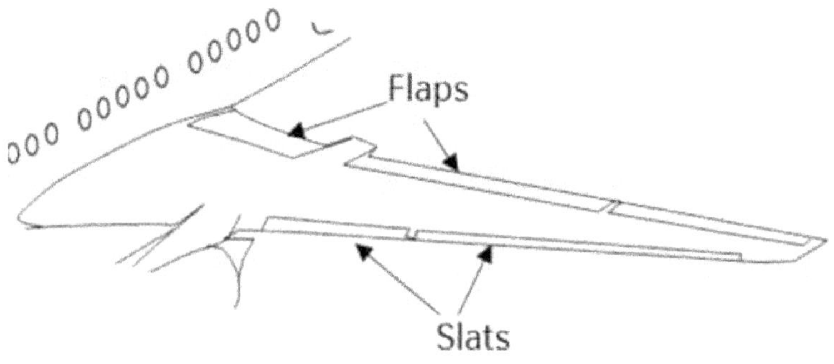

While these two devices fulfill the same function (increasing lift), they do so differently. In the first instance we must understand that the lift can be modified by angle of attack (AOA), wing curvature, wing surface and finally, speed.

On the one hand, SLATS works by modifying the angle of attack (AOA), thus modifying the lift. On the other hand, FLAPS works by modifying the curvature and wing surface, obtaining a modification in the value of the lift.

Let's start by analyzing the structure of SLATS. When this system is activated, the SLAT detaches from the leading edge by means of a mechanical actuator. This enables the wing airfoil to increase its angle of attack without producing a detachment of the airflow delaying the stall speed.

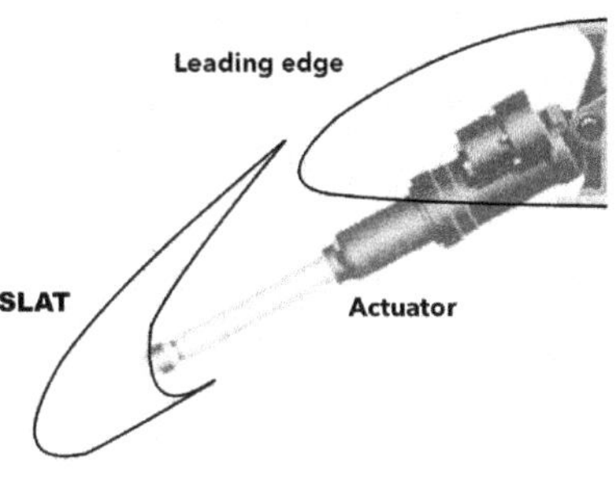

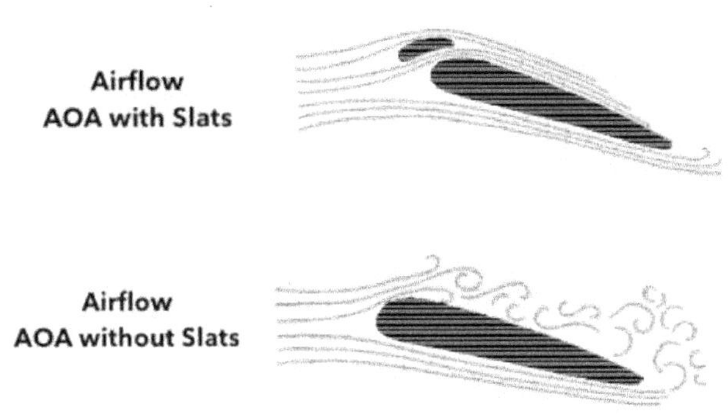

There are three types of slats, they can be fixed, automatic or manually operated.

Fixed slats: These devices remain in a fixed and extended position of the leading edge of the profile. On the one hand, they are useful since they do not depend on the pilot's actions. On the other hand, when they are always extended, during the cruise flight stage they present additional resistance to advance.

Automatic slats: These devices are configured to extend automatically at certain stages of flight where the plane is close to reaching a high angle of attack that approaches the stall speed.

Manual slats: This type of device allows the manual operation of the system from inside the cockpit, leaving its operation to the pilot's discretion.

In some particular cases, the slats system works in conjunction with the flaps system automatically. This is the case of the slats system of the AIRBUS 320 model, where when selecting the flaps lever at position 1, the aircraft system extends the slats and at the same time extends the flaps to their first position.

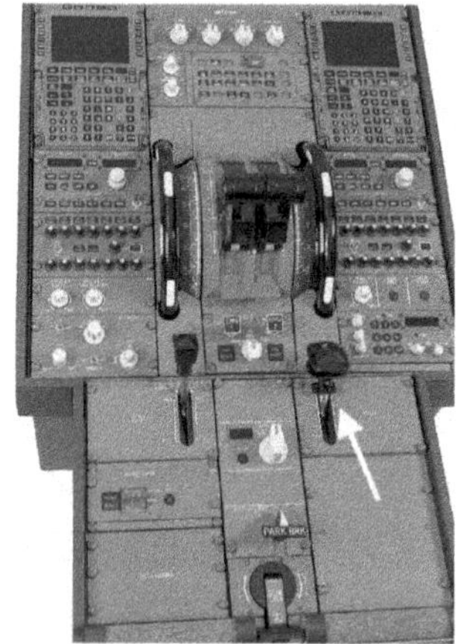

The flaps system can be located on the leading edge or at the trailing edge of the aircraft and are made up of aerodynamic surfaces or fins that extend from the respective edges in order to increase lift due to two variables:

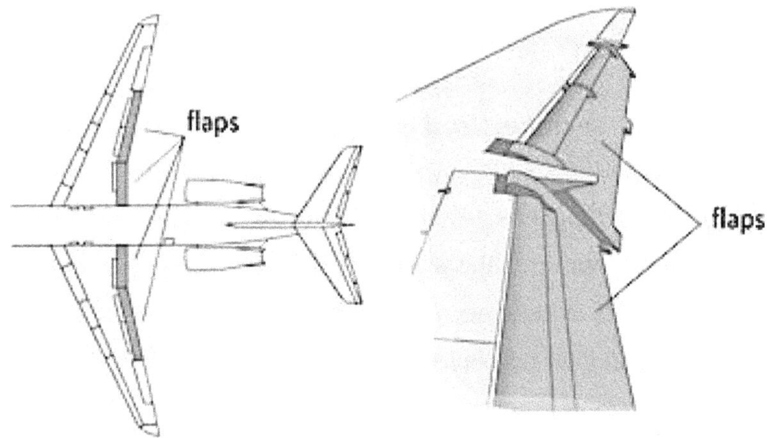

- ✓ By increasing the curvature of the wing airfoil, generating greater suction (lift) in the upper surface.
- ✓ By increasing the wing surface, modifying the variable "S" (surface) in the lifting formula and increasing its value.

The size of the FLAPS fins is measured by their curvature and represents 30% of the length of the wing curvature at most, that is, with FLAPS extended, the curvature of the wing increases its surface by an additional 30%. Depending on the purpose of the aircraft, the manufacturer may decide to install different models or types of FLAPS. Let's see the most used:

Simple: A flap system with a basic operating principle. The final section of the profile becomes a moving section and unfolds downwards. This type of FLAP is the most used in small general aviation.

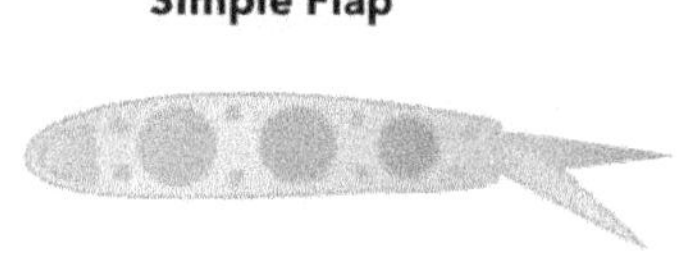

Lower surface: In this type of FLAPS, the profile remains complete and the FLAPS fin detaches from the lower surface. By maintaining the shape of the profile during its extension, the pitching movement it can generate is less.

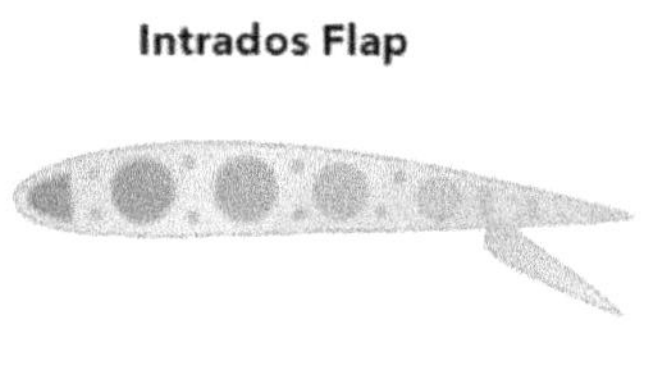

Slotted: This type of system has a groove between the FLAPS fin and the surface of the profile, allowing the flow of air to pass from the intrados to the extrados in order to stabilize the effects of the limit layer, where at the end of the wing profile it is usually transformed from laminar to turbulent.

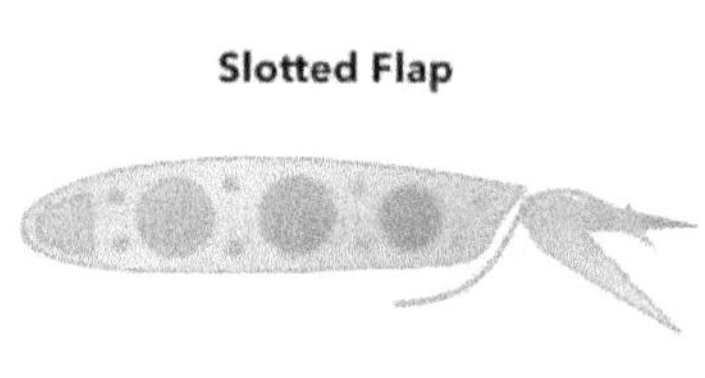

Fowler: Is considered the FLAPS system par excellence and presents different designs within the same system. In this type of FLAPS, the fin moves back and down in order to increase not only the curvature of the wing but also the wing surface.

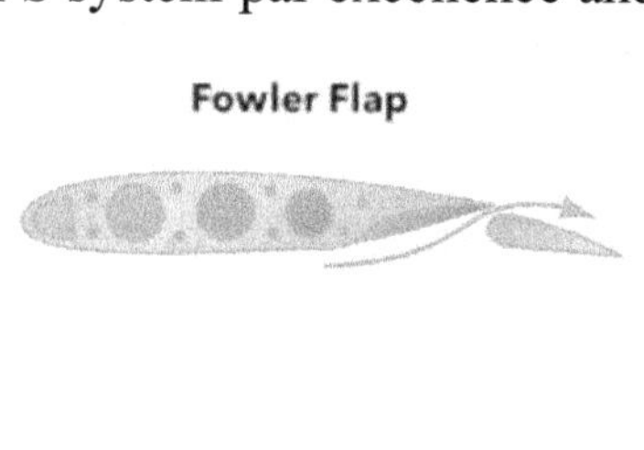

Multi Fowler: This type of system is the most used by large commercial aircrafts. Similar to the previous one but with a multi-fin system that male possible lifting to be improved.

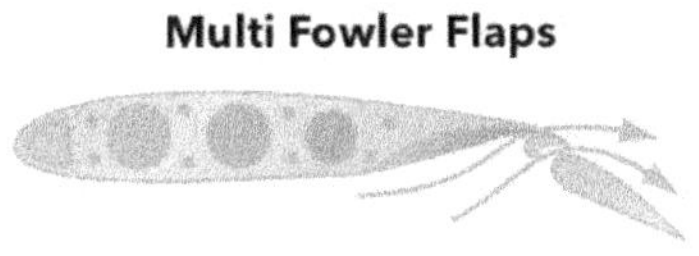

Finally, we find a FLAP system different from the rest located on the leading edge, similar to the SLATS system. It is known as FLAPS KRUEGER or usually called leading edge Flaps.

FLAP KRUEGER

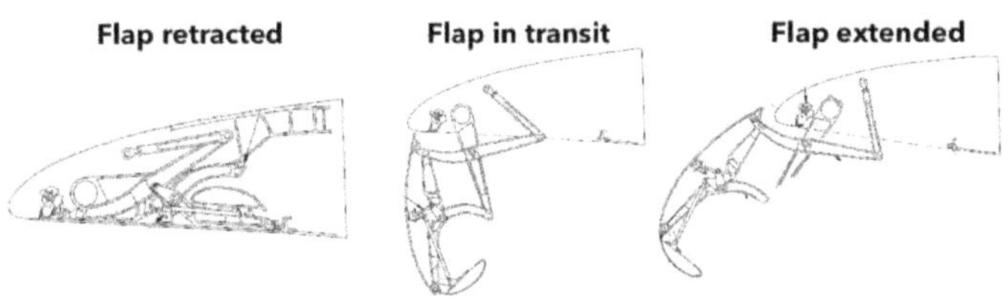

While the FLAPS KRUEGER system is similar to the SLATS system because it is located on the leading edge, the FLAP KRUEGER has additional aerodynamic benefits compared to the SLATS system. On the one hand, the FLAPS KRUEGER can fold completely to the leading edge as part of it without noticing differences. On the other hand the SLATS system, is a retraction system on the non-folding wing.

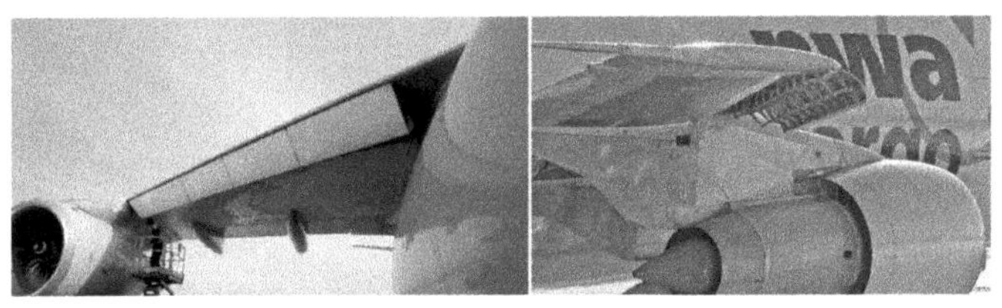

Similar to SLATS, the FLAPS system has an extension mechanism that varies depending on the type of FLAPS. The three most used extension mechanisms are the following:

Flap system extension

Extension by rail | **Extension by bars** | **Articulated extension**

Extension by rail: In this type of extension system, the path of the FLAP is uniform because it is mounted on a rail that leads it to the correct position and without deviations. Also, it is a system that has an additional weight and typical of the rails, which increases the weight of the plane.

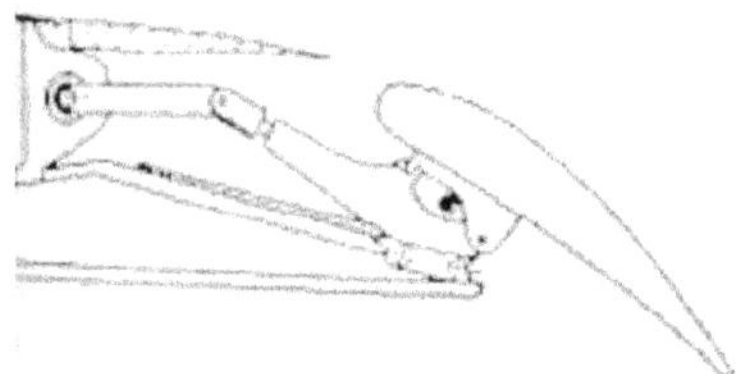

Extension by bars: A system similar to the previous one, but with a lower structural weight. A system used in simple types of FLAPS and mostly in low-performance aircrafts.

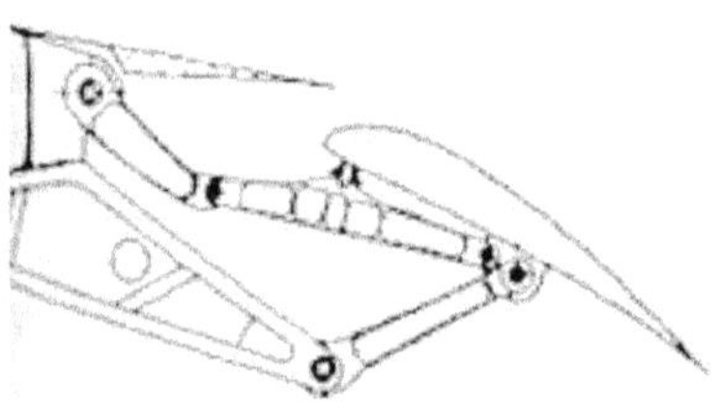

Articulated extension: A simple manufacturing system and low weight. The FLAP fin rotates over the same point to extend and withdraw.

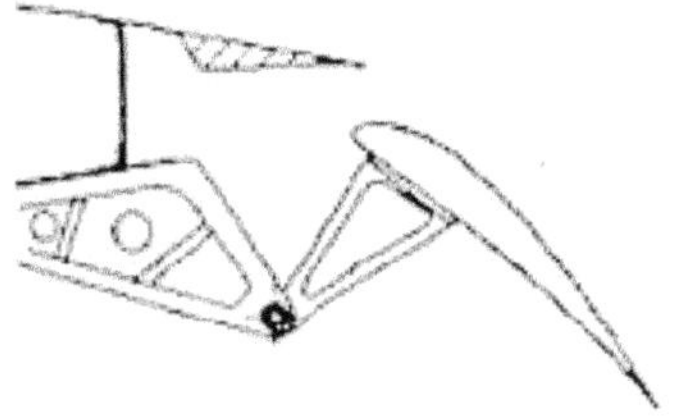

While the FLAPS extension types are defined by each manufacturer according to the design of their aircraft itself, there is the possibility that two different FLAPS extension systems coexist within the same aircraft design. This combination of extension systems is usually found in heavy aircraft of enormous wingspan.

Spoilers

They are considered as a lifting reduction system. This system is composed of aerodynamic surfaces mounted on the extrados on the wing surface and just in front of the Flaps. Its normal position is folded over the contour of the wing. By means of hydraulic activators, their drive leaves them in an almost vertical position and facing directly the relative wind.

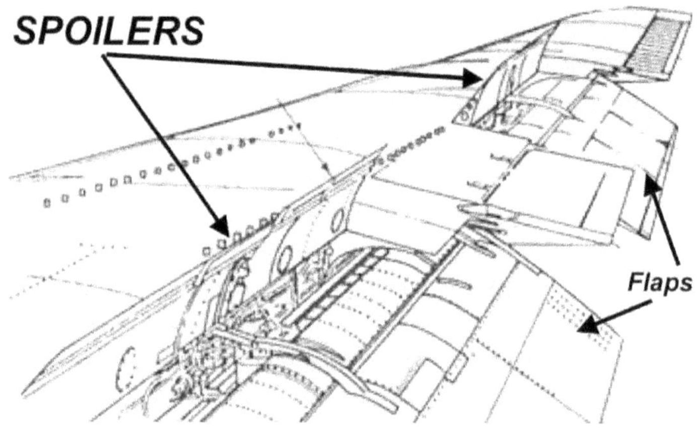

When spoilers are driven, they reduce lift and increase resistance in the location area of the device. Whether large or high performance aircraft, spoilers can fulfill three functions:

Balance: In this function the spoilers work together with the spoilers. When the aircraft's automatic system detects a certain inclination angle during a turn, it gradually activates the extension of the spoilers of the wing corresponding to the turn side. This action gives off the limit layer on the extrados of said wing, reduces lift and helps maximize the effect of the spoilers achieving a greater turn with less force load.

Air Brakes: When the spoiler system is manually operated, they extend over the wing between 30° and 35° perpendicular to it generating enormous resistance to advance, and with it, an immediate deceleration of the aircraft. This function is usually used in flight when you want to slow down quickly or when the aircraft requires a steeper descent without increasing its speed. Brakes are a manual function intentionally operated by pilots.

Landing: Unlike the previous function, in this case the spoilers extend over the wing between 50° and 60° perpendicular to it. The objective of this function is to reduce the landing stroke by breaking the boundary layer over the extrados and increasing the advance resistance of the aircraft. Additionally, the capacity of the braking system is greater since there is less lifting on the extrados due to the opening of its limit layer, the wheels of the plane tend to remain firmer on the runway.

Biblioteca
Aeronáutica
aviación en simples pasos

Chapter 2

Landing gear

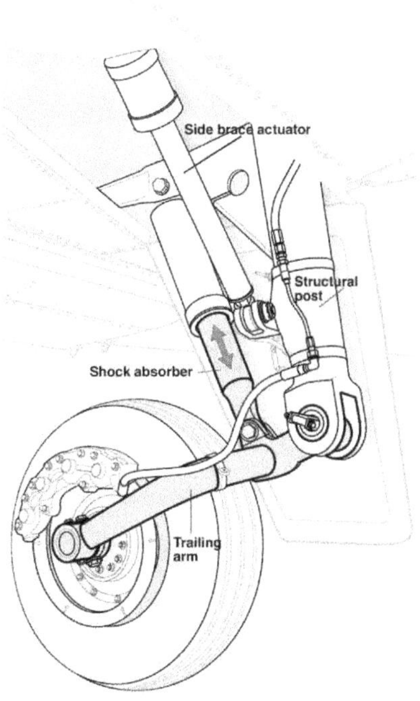

Biblioteca
Aeronáutica
aviación en simples pasos

Landing gear

The functions of the landing gear are, firstly, to provide a means for maneuvering the aircraft on the ground, secondly, to support the aircraft at a convenient height to allow clearance for propellers, flaps, etc., and thirdly, to absorb the kinetic energy of landing.

Once in the air, the landing gear serves no useful purpose and becomes dead weight. While it is possible to perform all maneuvers considering the drag generated by the landing gear wheels, it is necessary to reduce their impact on deceleration caused by the wind hitting the structure. For this reason, extensive research has been conducted into landing gear unit designs to reduce both weight and storage volume when retracted.

In light aircraft and some larger ones, where simplicity is of utmost importance, fixed (non-retractable) landing gear is often installed. For example, in light aircraft and trainers, the lower performance caused by the drag of the fixed landing gear during flight is compensated by its simplicity, lower maintenance, and reduced initial cost. In faster aircraft, drag becomes increasingly important, so the landing

gear is retracted into the wings or fuselage during flight. However, this system involves added weight, increased complexity, and additional maintenance with retractable landing gear.

Fixed landing gear

The first distinction in landing gear models is the wheel arrangement. Here, the system is divided into two main groups: conventional landing gear, designed with two main wheels at the front and a smaller wheel at the rear of the aircraft, and tricycle landing gear, designed with a nose wheel that guides the aircraft's taxiing direction and two wheels located midway, responsible for absorbing the impact pressure (shock absorption).

There are three main types of fixed landing gear: those with spring steel struts, those employing rubber cords for impact absorption (shock absorption), and those with oleo-pneumatic systems for impact absorption (shock absorption).

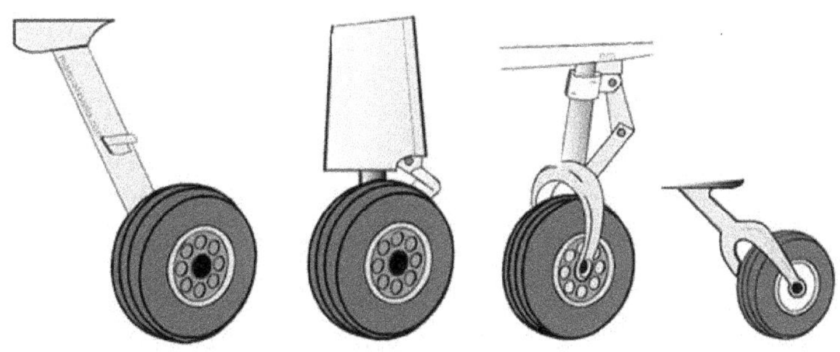

Spring steel struts: Spring steel struts are generally used in the main landing gear positions. The strut consists of a conical spring steel tube or strip, with the upper end bolted to the fuselage and the lower end terminating in an axle, onto which the wheel and brake are mounted. Both main wheels support the aircraft on the surface, exerting pressure on the struts, which allows for slight separation from the initial position, cushioning the impact.

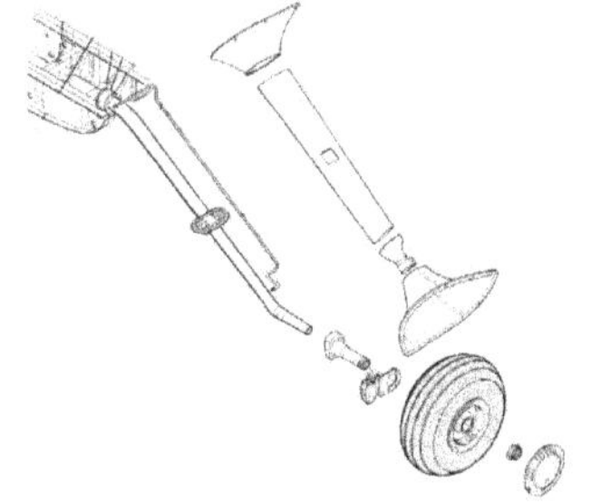

Rubber cords: When rubber cords are used as shock absorbers, the landing gear usually takes the form of tubular bars, designed and installed so that the landing force is directed against a series of rubber loops or eyes. This is an older system used in early landing gear models, offering significant benefits in terms of low maintenance and repair simplicity.

Oleo-pneumatic system: Some fixed main landing gear, and most fixed nose gears, are equipped with an oleo-pneumatic shock-absorbing strut or tube. The design of oleo-pneumatic struts varies considerably. Some may be fitted with fairings to reduce drag, while others may simply present their entire structure exposed, increasing the effect of parasitic drag.

Fairings can be installed on the landing gear to reduce drag. One disadvantage of their use is that they can collect mud when landing or taking off from grass or dirt airstrips. This can significantly increase the aircraft's weight and may affect takeoff performance. To avoid this situation, if any mud has accumulated, it must be removed, and the fairings should be cleaned or replaced before the next takeoff.

Nose gear

The nose gear typically has a lighter structure than the main gear units since it bears less weight and is usually only subjected to direct compression loads. The nose wheel must be able to rotate freely. Nosewheel steering allows the wheel to turn from side to side in response to differential braking of the main wheels.

A steering mechanism is required to allow the pilot to safely maneuver the aircraft on the ground. Early methods involved differential braking and freely castoring nose wheels, but today, most light aircraft feature nose wheels that are directly steered by the rudder pedals from within the cockpit.

On aircraft equipped with conventional landing gear, this nosewheel steering system is not available. In these cases, the pilot must steer the aircraft by applying pressure on the pedals to change the direction of the rudder.

Due to the flexibility of the tire sidewalls, a rapid, unstable, sinusoidal oscillation or vibration, known as shimmy, can be induced in the main landing gear parts during taxiing. Excessive shimmy, especially at high speeds, can set off vibrations throughout the aircraft, increasing the level of danger. Worn wheel bearings and uneven tire pressures can increase the tendency for shimmy to occur.

Shimmy can be reduced in several ways, such as by installing an anti-shimmy damper or by using strong self-centering springs on the nosewheel control rod. Some larger aircraft are equipped with dual nose wheels, as it has been proven that paired wheels (i.e., dual wheels) are effective in minimizing shimmy effects.

Cessna 172 Landing gear

The Cessna C-172 model features a tricycle-type landing gear with a steerable nose wheel and two fixed main wheels located just below the cockpit. Depending on the model, the landing gear may be equipped with wheel fairings to reduce drag or simply have the wheels exposed to the airflow.

The characteristics of the landing gear are divided between the nose wheel and what is known as the main gear or main wheels. Starting with the main gear, it is connected to the fuselage via a steel arm that functions as both a support and a shock absorber. Each main wheel is equipped with a hydraulic disc brake system and may be covered by an aerodynamic structure in some models.

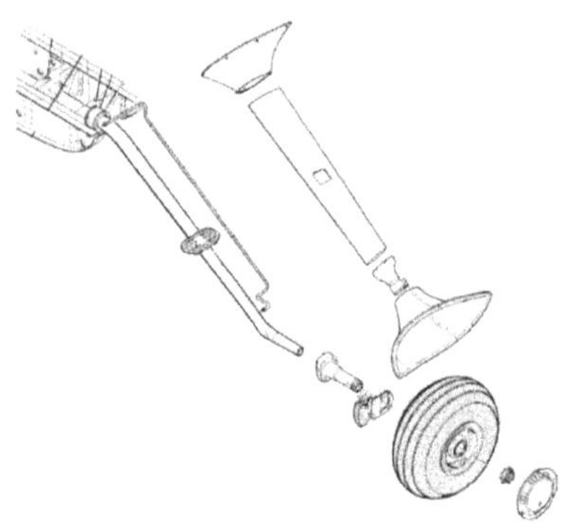

On the other hand, the nose gear has two very important characteristics: a shock-absorbing system and a wheel steering system. The latter is directly linked to the operation of the pedals from the cockpit, which act on the aircraft's rudder. The shock absorption of the nose gear is one of the key features of this system. Its principle of operation is quite simple; it relies on a hydraulic system involving two air- or nitrogen-pressurized chambers and a set of springs that work together to provide smooth and impact-resistant damping. It is common in such systems for the shock absorber to "deflate," as is often mentioned in the jargon. This

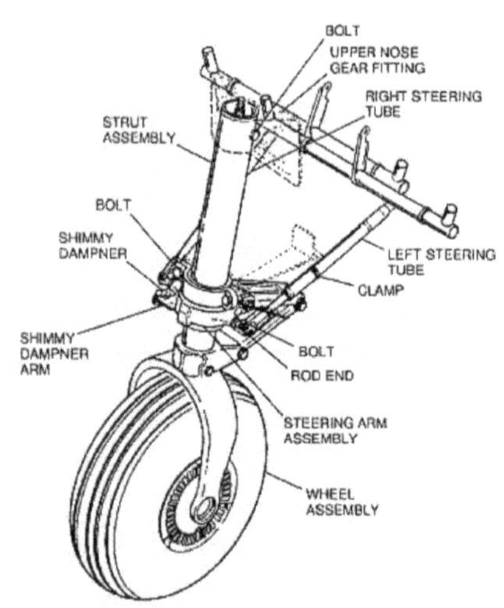

means that the shock absorber has lost the circulating air within the system and no longer has the ability to travel up and down, resting completely on the wheel fork.

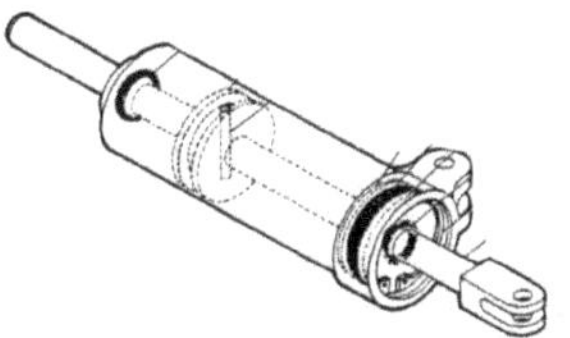

Another fundamental characteristic of the nose gear is its ability to steer the wheel by operating the pedals from the cockpit. This function is known as "Nose Wheel Steering." Its operation is very straightforward; it involves a connection between the pedal action from the cockpit and the fork of the landing gear structure. When the pedal is pressed to one side, the fork will turn in that direction to steer the movement during taxiing.

Finally, another quality of the nose gear is the "Vibration Dampening System" known as the "Shimmy Damper." This consists of a drum filled with hydraulic fluid that absorbs the impact forces on the landing gear fork. This unique system allows for smoother taxiing with reduced vibrations, which is particularly useful when operating on grass or dirt surfaces, where the nose gear would experience greater vibrations than on a flat surface.

For the entire range of low-performance single-engine aircraft, Cessna has developed a manual towing system utilizing a bar connected to the nose gear fork or directly to the wheel surface, enabling an operator to push the aircraft and steer the nose wheel manually through the force applied.

When a tow bar is not available, Cessna recommends turning the aircraft by applying pressure on the horizontal stabilizer to lift the nose of the aircraft, allowing it to be turned towards the desired direction.

Retractable landing gear

An increasing number of light aircraft are equipped with retractable landing gear to reduce drag, thereby improving the aircraft's performance. Retraction is typically accomplished through a hydraulic system, though pneumatic or electric systems are also used. In some cases, energy is used solely for retraction, while extension is affected by gravity and gliding drag.

The retractable landing gear is also equipped with mechanical locks to ensure that each gear leg is securely locked in either the retracted or extended position. Retractable landing gear systems also include devices to indicate to the pilot the position of each section of the gear, as well as a means to manually extend the gear in the event of a power failure. Furthermore, safety systems are provided to prevent retraction of the landing gear while the aircraft is on the ground and to prevent landings with the landing gear retracted.

The retraction movement of the landing gear varies depending on the design of each manufacturer. In some cases, the wheels of the main gear retract and stow within the wings, while in other cases, they are housed within the fuselage. The nose wheel will always be stowed within the fuselage, with its travel varying forward or backward depending on the aircraft.

Landing gear tires

Aircraft wheels are equipped with tires that generally consist of both an inner rubber tube and an outer cover. The inner tube is inflated with compressed air to absorb shocks and support the weight of the aircraft. The cover protects the inner tube from damage, maintains the tire's shape, transmits braking forces, and provides a wear surface.

The tire cover consists of a rubber casing reinforced with layers of cotton or nylon cords. The cords are not woven but arranged parallel in individual layers and bonded together with a thin film of rubber that prevents adjacent layers from cutting into each other as the tire flexes. During the construction of the cover, the layers are paired.

Each pair is called a pocket, established such that the cords of adjacent layers are at 90 degrees to each other; this is called a bias ply. Tire manufacturers assign a ply rating to each tire. This rating does not directly relate to the number of plies in the tire but is an index of the tire's strength. To absorb and distribute load shocks, two narrow layers embedded in thick rubber layers are located between the casing and the tread; these special layers are called breaker strips.

The casing is held at the rim of the wheel by interweaving the layers around non-stretchable steel wire beads to form ply overlaps. This part of the cover is known as the bead.

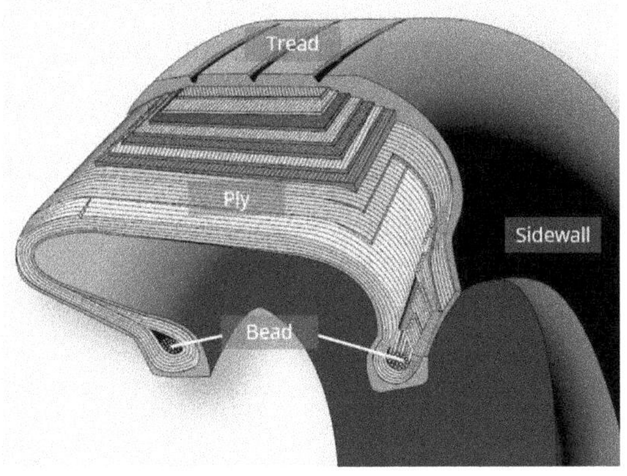

The size of a tire is marked on its sidewall, including the outer diameter, inner diameter, and width of the tire, all in inches.

The ply rating, an index of tire strength, is also marked on the sidewall. Typically, the ply rating is shown as an abbreviation, such as PR16, but it may also be fully displayed as "16 PLY RATING." The tire speed rating, indicating the maximum speed for which the tire is designed, is printed on a panel on the sidewall of some high-speed tires. This rating takes into account altitude pressure, ambient temperature, and wind component, allowing the calculation of the maximum takeoff weight that the tires can support.

Green or gray dots painted on the tire's sidewall indicate the position of the vent holes. These vents prevent air pressure from being trapped between layers, which could cause the tire casing to rupture when exposed to low pressures experienced during high-altitude flight. A red dot or triangle indicates the lightest part of the tire. If positioned next to the valve during tire fitting, this helps balance the wheel assembly.

Additional tire considerations

Tires must be protected from excessive heat, moisture, bright sunlight, and contact with oil, fuel, and hydraulic fluid, as these can adversely affect rubber. Any liquid inadvertently spilled or dripping onto a tire should be cleaned immediately.

When tires are first mounted on a wheel, they tend to shift slightly around the rim. This phenomenon is known as "creep" and is considered normal at this stage. However, after the tires settle, this movement should cease. It is less likely to occur if the tire air pressure is maintained correctly. To assist with this, tire manufacturers specify a nominal inflation pressure for each tire.

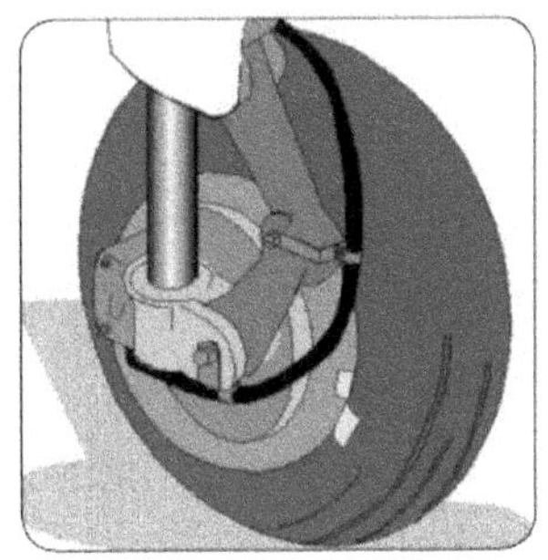

Witness marks are painted on the side of the wheel. When the tire is first fitted to the wheel, the reference marks will align with each other. However, for various reasons, including hard landings, heavy braking, and low tire pressures, the tire may move around the wheel, causing the witness marks to become misaligned.

During pre-flight inspection, tires should be checked for cuts, bulges, embedded stones, metal, or glass, signs of wear, creep, etc. Cuts in the tire cover that penetrate to the cords render the tire unserviceable. The cords will be recognizable as pieces of white fibrous material embedded in the rubber. Bulges may indicate a partial failure of the casing. If the fabric fractures, the tire should be replaced.

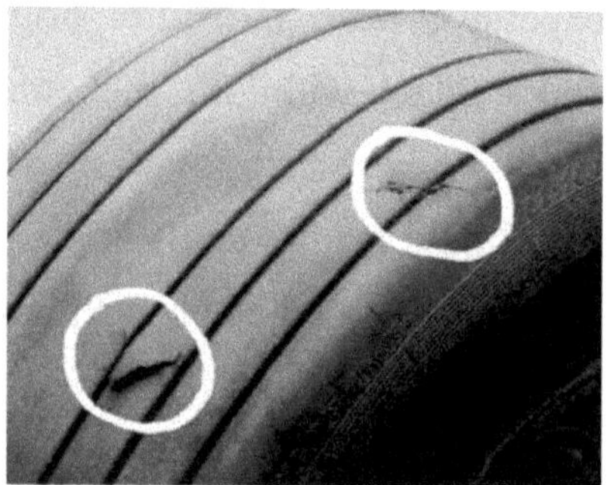

Landing gear brakes

Like most braking systems, aircraft wheel brakes operate by using friction between a fixed surface and a moving one to bring an aircraft to a stop, converting kinetic energy into thermal energy in the process. The amount of heat generated to stop even a light aircraft is extremely large. The larger the aircraft, the greater the heat generated. Most light aircraft now use hydraulic disc brakes as a means to decelerate or stop. These use a series of fixed friction pads, with bearings or grip, against a rotating disc, similar to car disc brakes. The friction pads are made of inorganic friction material, and the discs are forged steel with a specially hardened surface.

When pressure is applied to the brake pedals or handbrake lever, hydraulic pressure builds up in the cylinder behind the piston. This pressure moves the piston within the caliper unit, pushing the brake pad against the brake disc.

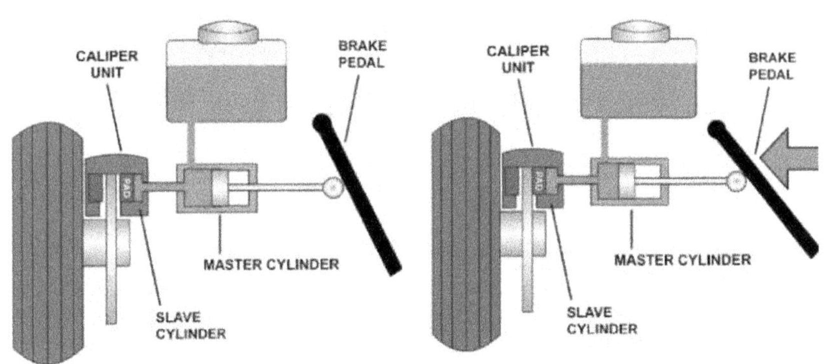

The reaction of the inner brake pad pushing against the disc will cause the caliper unit to move in the opposite direction to the piston, bringing the outer brake pad along until the disc is pinched between the two pads.

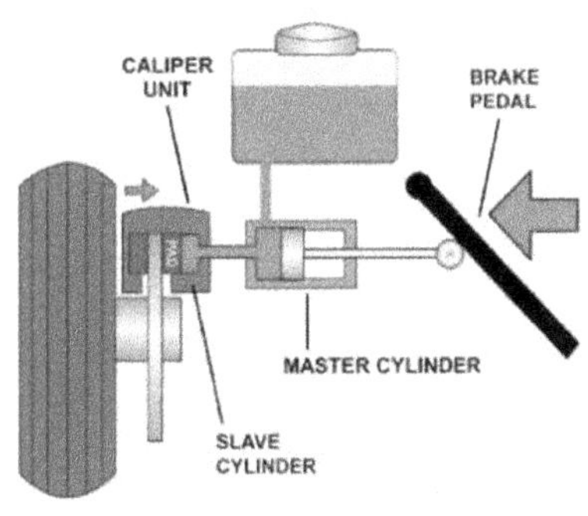

The force applied to the brake pads will be proportional to the effort applied to the brakes. The brakes can be applied together, or, if differential braking is required to maneuver the aircraft in tight spaces, the brakes can be used separately.

Most light aircraft have a manual parking brake. When engaged, the handbrake locks the hydraulic pressure applied by the foot brakes.

Chapter 3

Propellers

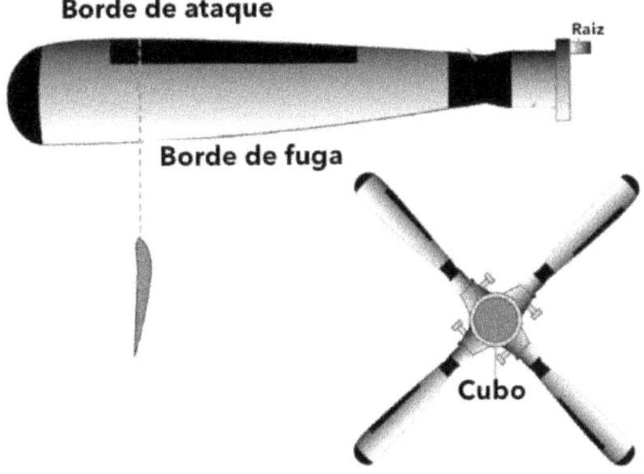

Biblioteca
Aeronáutica
aviación en simples pasos

Propellers

Most general aviation aircraft operate with propellers to generate thrust. The purpose of a propeller is to convert the power supplied by an engine into propulsive thrust. The detailed theory of how thrust is produced is complex, but simply put, there are two principles that explain the nature of thrust:

The propeller accelerates a mass of air backward, and according to Newton's third law, it experiences a force acting on itself in the opposite direction. This force is called thrust.

The blades of the propeller are aerodynamic profiles that act as rotating wings, causing a difference in static pressure across the blades. Just as a wing generates a lift force acting upward, the propeller generates a forward horizontal force known as thrust.

The airflow over a propeller is more complex than over a wing, as the propeller not only rotates but also moves forward. Some aerodynamic analysts believe that the two aforementioned principles of propeller thrust are interconnected and can be explained by Newton's second law, in the sense that the rotating blades of the propeller impart a rate of change of momentum to the air flowing over the blades, thus applying a force to the air and changing its speed and pressure distribution.

Blades

The propeller consists of two or more aerodynamically shaped blades attached to a central hub. This hub is mounted on a propeller shaft driven by the engine. The entire assembly is rotated by the propeller shaft. Similar to a wing, the blade of the propeller has a root and a tip, a leading edge and a trailing edge, and a curved cross-section whose mean aerodynamic chord extends from the center of the leading edge radius to the trailing edge.

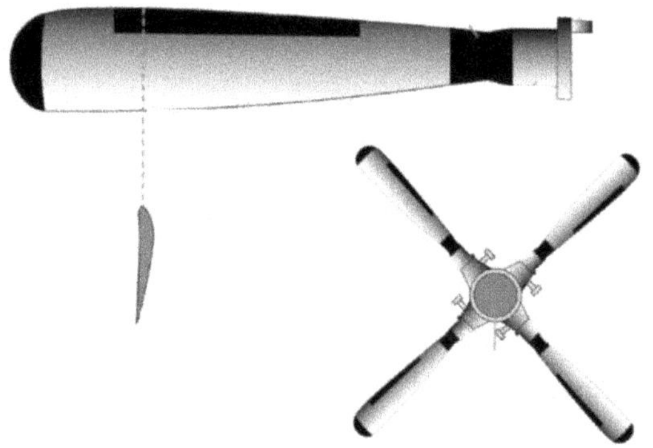

The blade chord line is a straight line connecting the centers of curvature of the leading and trailing edges. It represents the distance between these edges.

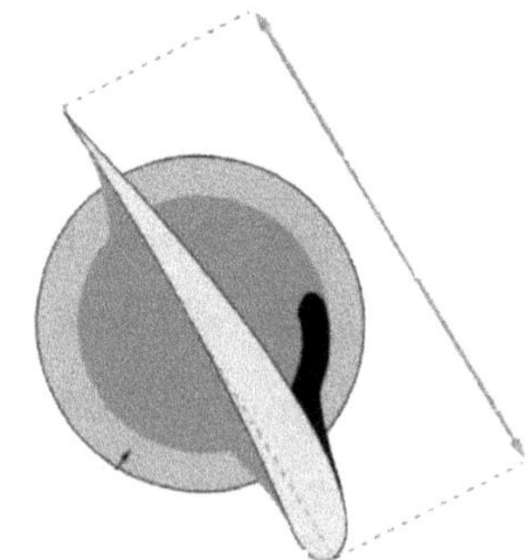

The pitch of the blade is the angle between the chord line and the axis of the hub. The pitch decreases from the root to the tip of the blade, as the rotational speed increases from root to tip. This variation along the length of the blade ensures an optimal angle of attack. For reference, the blade angle is measured at a point 75% along the length from the root.

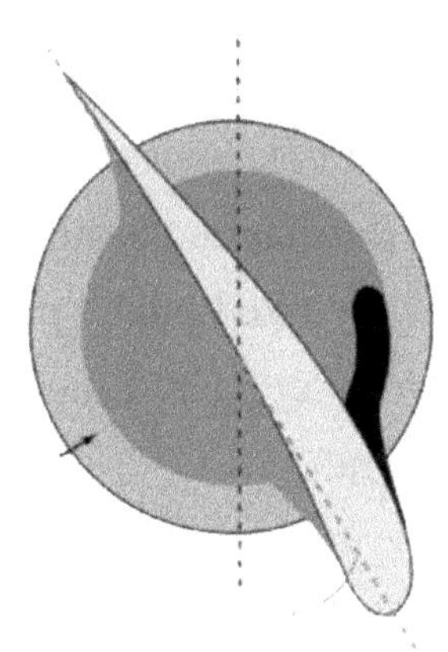

The sections of the blade near the tip of the propeller are further from the propeller axis and travel a greater distance for each rotation. Therefore, for any given engine speed (measured in revolutions per minute or RPM), the rotational speed at the tip of the propeller is greater than that of the elements of the blade near the hub. The blade angle determines the geometric pitch of the propeller. A small blade angle is referred to as fine pitch, while a large blade angle is called coarse pitch.

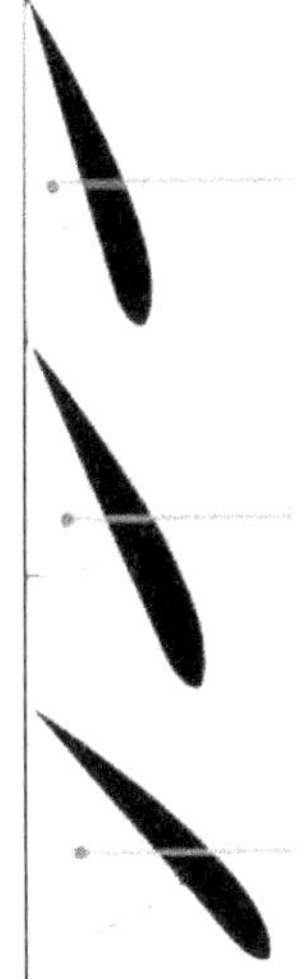

The angle between the blade's chord line and the relative airflow during propeller rotation is known as the angle of attack, shown in the diagram as alpha (α). The angle of attack of a fixed-pitch propeller depends on the propeller's RPM and the forward speed of the aircraft.

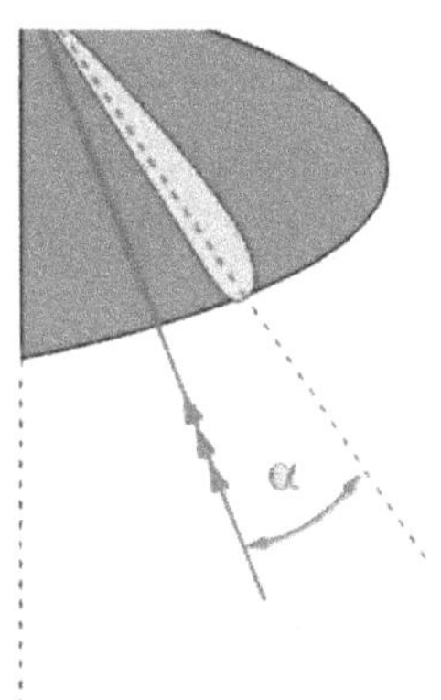

Propeller efficiency

A propeller must be capable of absorbing all the shaft power generated by the engine and must operate with maximum efficiency across the entire performance envelope required by the aircraft. At any given engine speed, measured in revolutions per minute (RPM), the larger the propeller's diameter, the greater the tip speed would be. For example, at 2,600 RPM, a propeller with an 8-foot (2.5-meter) diameter would have a tip speed of 653 miles per hour, approaching the speed of sound at sea level.

A large diameter propeller would be an effective "absorber" of engine power. However, a critical factor in propeller efficiency is tip speed. If the tip speed is too high, the blade tips will approach the speed of sound, and compressibility effects will reduce thrust and increase rotational drag. Supersonic tip speeds will greatly reduce the efficiency of a propeller and significantly increase the noise it generates. This factor imposes limits on the propeller's diameter, RPM, and the speeds that can be achieved by propeller-driven aircraft. Another limitation on the propeller's diameter is the need to maintain adequate ground clearance.

To increase power absorption, various propeller characteristics can be considered beyond the diameter. The usual method is to increase the "solidity" of the propeller. Propeller solidity is the ratio of the total frontal area of the blades to the propeller disc area. One way to increase solidity is by increasing the blade's chord. This increases solidity, but reduces the blade's aspect ratio, making the propeller less efficient.

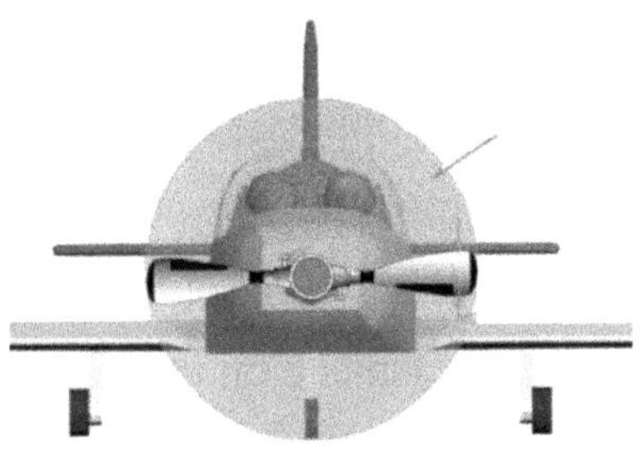

Secondly, the number of blades can be increased. This increases power absorption without increasing tip speed or reducing aspect ratio. This method is typically used to increase propeller solidity. However, increasing the number of blades beyond a certain point (five or six) will reduce overall efficiency.

Nonetheless, thrust is generated by accelerating air rearward. Therefore, making the propeller disc too solid reduces the mass of air that can flow through and be accelerated by the propeller. To efficiently increase the number of blades, contra-rotating propellers can be used—two propellers that rotate in opposite directions on the same axis. However, contra-rotating propellers are only practical on aircraft with very powerful engines.

Forces generated by the propeller

Due to its rotation, a propeller generates yaw, roll, and pitch moments. These are caused by several factors, such as torque reaction, gyroscopic precession, the slipstream effect, and asymmetric blade effects.

Torque Reaction: If the propeller rotates clockwise, the equal and opposite torque reaction will create a counterclockwise rolling moment around the aircraft's longitudinal axis. During takeoff, this will apply more load to the left main wheel, increasing rolling resistance on the left wheel, causing the aircraft to yaw left.

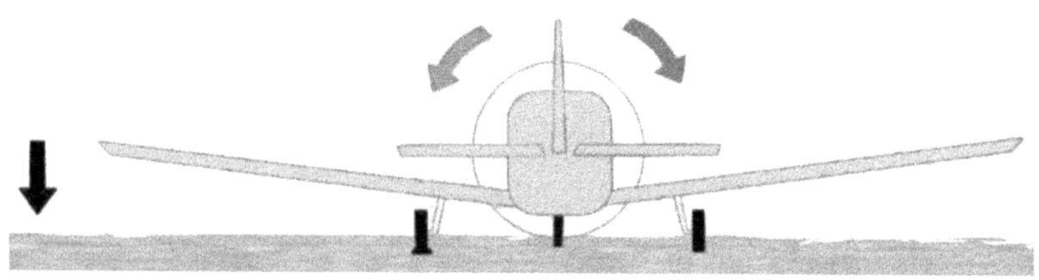

In flight, torque reaction will also cause the aircraft to roll left with a clockwise-rotating propeller. This effect is particularly noticeable when full power is applied to initiate a climb. Obviously, for a counterclockwise-rotating propeller, all the effects described in this section will act in the opposite direction. Low airspeeds will reduce the effectiveness of control surfaces in counteracting the roll moment caused by torque. Torque reaction can be eliminated by installing contra-rotating propellers. The torque from the two propellers, rotating in opposite directions on the same axis, will cancel each other out. However, the cost of such a solution is high, and it is only suitable for very high-power engines.

Gyroscopic Effect: A rotating propeller has the properties of a gyroscope: rigidity in space and precession. The property that produces what is known as the gyroscopic effect is precession. Gyroscopic precession refers to the effect that occurs when a force is applied to the edge of a rotating disc. When a force is applied to the edge of a rotating propeller disc, the force's effect is felt at a point 90° ahead in the direction of rotation and in the same direction as the applied force.

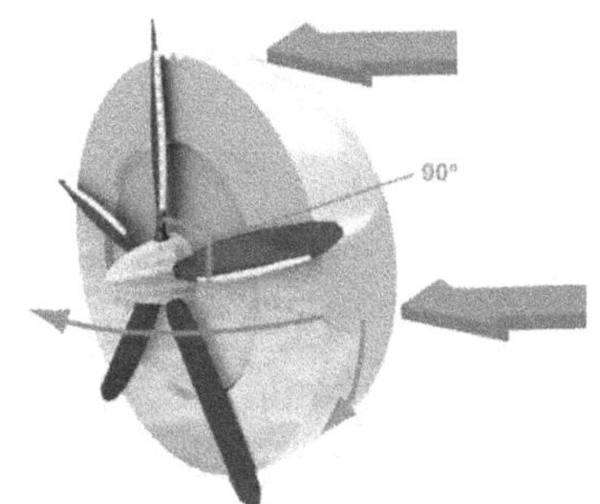

As the aircraft pitches up or down or rolls left or right, a force is applied to the edge of the rotating propeller disc. For example, if an aircraft with a counterclockwise-rotating propeller (as seen from the cockpit) pitches down, the aircraft behaves as though a forward force is applied to the top of the propeller disc. However, the effective line of action of this force acts 90° ahead in the direction of rotation, causing the aircraft to yaw to the right. The gyroscopic effect can be easily determined when considering the point of application of the force on the propeller disc.

Slipstream Effect: As the propeller rotates, it produces a rearward airflow or slipstream that spirals around the aircraft. This spiraling slipstream causes a change in airflow around the rudder. In the case shown here, due to the clockwise rotation of the propeller, the spiraling slipstream strikes the rudder at an angle from the left, producing a rightward lateral force, inducing a left yaw.

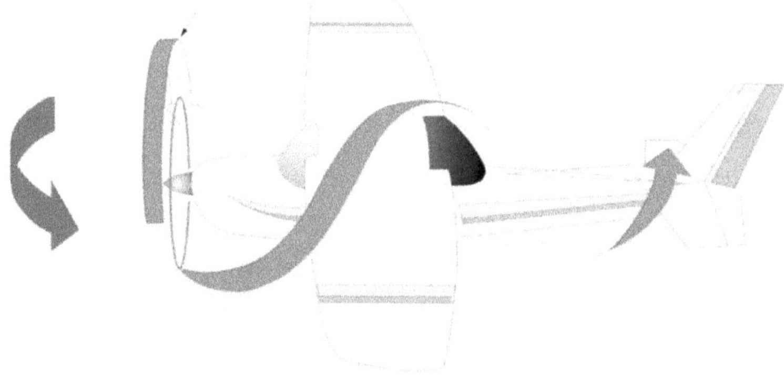

The amount of rotation given to the air depends on the power setting. The slipstream effect can be reduced with the following considerations: a small fixed tab on the rudder, a slightly right-offset engine thrust line, or rudder trim compensation.

Asymmetric Effect: During takeoff or landing in a tailwheel aircraft, the axis of the propeller will tilt upward relative to the horizontal. As a result, as the aircraft moves forward, the descending blade of the rotating propeller covers a larger path than the ascending blade for each rotation. This fact means that the linear speed of the descending blade is greater than that of the ascending blade, and its angle of attack is also higher. Therefore, the descending blade will generate more thrust than the ascending blade. The thrust differential on the two sides of the propeller disc will generate a left rolling moment for a clockwise-rotating propeller. The asymmetric blade effect will be more pronounced at full power and low airspeed with a high angle of attack.

Wooden propellers

Wooden propellers are the basic type that has been used in aviation since the first flight of the Wright Flyer I at Kitty Hawk to the present day in small light aircraft, such as the Piper PA-11, as well as in many ultralight and experimental aircraft. These are fixed-pitch propellers that equip engines with a maximum power of 90 hp. Wooden propellers are components that require extreme quality control, both of the raw material and during the manufacturing process. The construction of these propellers is a handcrafted process that considers the number of knots and grain of the wood; complex procedures of gluing, sealing, and turning are employed to achieve the necessary dimensions and weights.

Metal propellers

Metal propellers have been the most widely used, even to this day. They equip light aircraft such as the Cessna 150, the classic Douglas DC-3, and current turboprop aircraft like the Raytheon Beechcraft B200. They can be either fixed-pitch, similar to those used on light aircraft, or variable-pitch. The metal propeller consists of a central hub that houses each of the blades. Variable-pitch propellers have a mechanism that allows angular movement of each blade during flight... we will develop this concept further later. Both the blades and the hub are made from aluminum alloys that provide a good balance of mechanical strength, weight, and flexibility.

Composite propellers

We could say that composite propellers are the technological evolution of metal propellers. Their structure, function, and arrangement are similar to those of metal propellers; however, they possess a significantly lower weight with aerodynamic performance above the average of metal propellers. The structure consists of a metal hub made of aluminum alloy and blades manufactured with lightweight cores, internal structural reinforcements, and a covering made of composite fibers (various types of carbon fibers are commonly used). There are composite propellers that combine a carbon covering with a core made of various types of wood.

These types of propellers are used by modern high-performance turboprop aircraft. They possess adaptability and performance characteristics that allow for more efficient propulsion of large aircraft such as the military transport Airbus A400, as well as medium transport aircraft like the Saab 2000, among others.

Operating principles of propellers

As mentioned in the earlier paragraphs, a propeller is a relatively simple assembly consisting of a hub and a combination of blades.

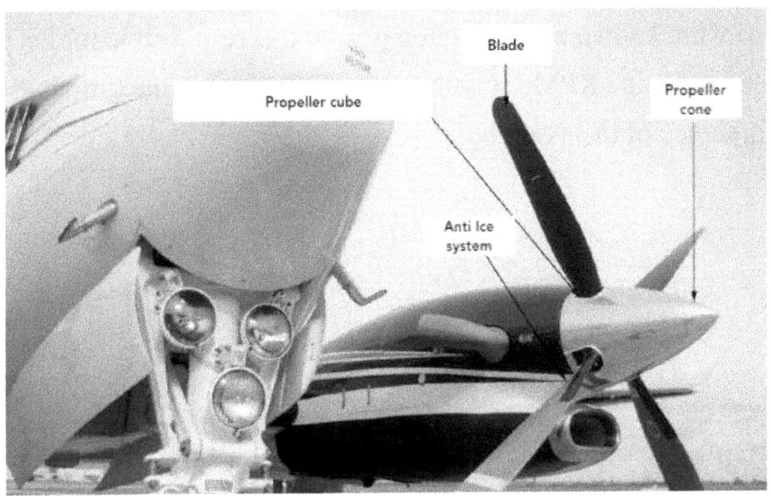

The aerodynamic profiles that make up a propeller are subject to the same laws and principles as any other aerodynamic profile, such as an aircraft wing. Each of these profiles, in this case the blades, has an angle of attack relative to the relative wind acting on the blade, which is close to the plane of revolution of the propeller, and a pitch (equal to the angle of incidence).

The rotation of the propeller, akin to many small wings rotating, accelerates the airflow toward the trailing edge of each profile while pushing it backward (similar to what occurs with a wing). This process results in the backward acceleration of a large mass of air, creating a reaction force that propels the aircraft forward.

A critical point in blade design is the speed at which the tips rotate, as if the rotational speed approaches the speed of sound, there is a significant decrease in performance. This fact imposes limits on the diameter and RPM at which propellers can operate, which is why some aircraft incorporate a reduction mechanism based on gears or pulleys between the engine output shaft and the propeller. This mechanism, known as a reduction gearbox, is responsible for keeping the propeller's RPM within safe limits and maximizing the performance of the assembly.

The thrust force of the aircraft is directly related to the amount of air it moves and the speed at which it accelerates that air; therefore, it depends on the size of the propeller, its pitch, and its rotational speed, as well as its design, shape, number of blades, diameter, etc. Beyond the number of blades, propellers are primarily classified into fixed-pitch and variable-pitch (constant-speed and variable-speed) propellers. The pitch of a propeller refers to the angle formed by the chord of the blade profiles with the plane of rotation of the propeller.

It is important to remember that pitch is not the same as blade angle. Although these terms are often used interchangeably, pitch is influenced by the blade angle; this difference is known as geometric pitch and effective pitch. The slip of the propeller defines the difference between geometric pitch and effective pitch. Geometric pitch is the distance a propeller should theoretically advance in one revolution, disregarding aerodynamic slip, while effective pitch is the actual distance traveled.

Thus, the relationship between the two can be expressed as:

Geometric pitch - Effective pitch = Slip

Although the blade angle and the pitch of the propeller are closely related, the blade angle is the angle between the face or chord of a section of the blade and the plane in which the propeller rotates. The line of the blade chord of the propeller is determined in a manner similar to the chord line of an aerodynamic profile. In fact, a propeller blade can be considered as composed of an infinite number of thin blade elements, each representing a miniature aerodynamic section whose chord is the width of the propeller blade at that section.

A typical propeller blade can be described as an aerodynamic surface subjected to irregular torsion. For better understanding, a blade can be divided into segments (stations similar to those used in theoretical fuselage divisions) located by station numbers in inches from the center. In the graph shown below, the effect of torsion along the blade, the change in thickness, and the characteristics of the aerodynamic profile throughout the component can be seen simply (ref. graph adapted from the Federal Aviation Administration document FAA-H-8083-32-AMT). The distances are referenced in inches.

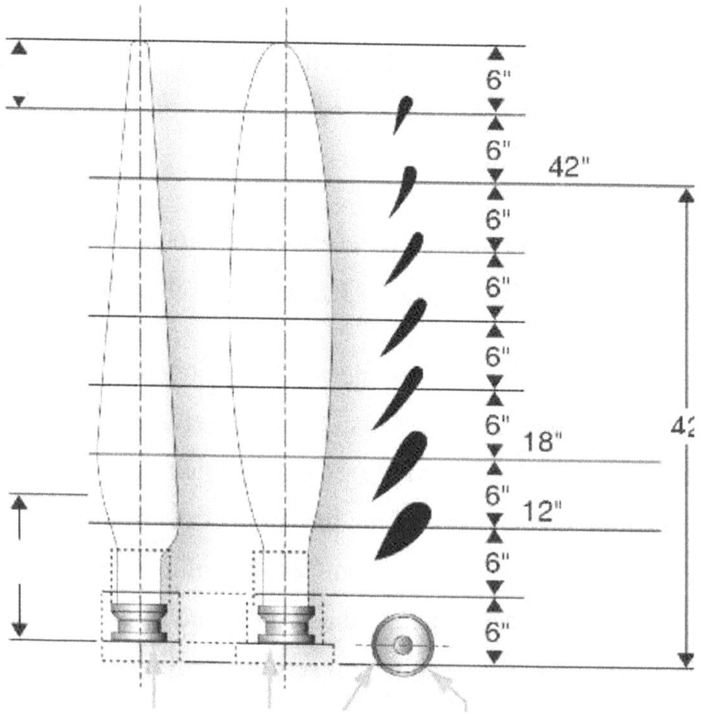

Next, let's explore the particularities of each type of propeller and their applications.

Fixed pitch propellers

In this type of propeller, the pitch is determined by the aircraft designer's best judgment and cannot be changed by the pilot. This pitch is fixed for all flight regimes, which restricts and limits its effectiveness; a propeller optimized for takeoff or climb is not as efficient at cruise speed, and vice versa. A fixed-pitch propeller is akin to a single-speed transmission; it compensates for its lack of efficiency with great simplicity of operation.

In aircraft equipped with low-power engines, the propeller is usually of reduced diameter and is directly fixed as an extension of the crankshaft. Therefore, the RPM of the propeller is the same as that of the engine.

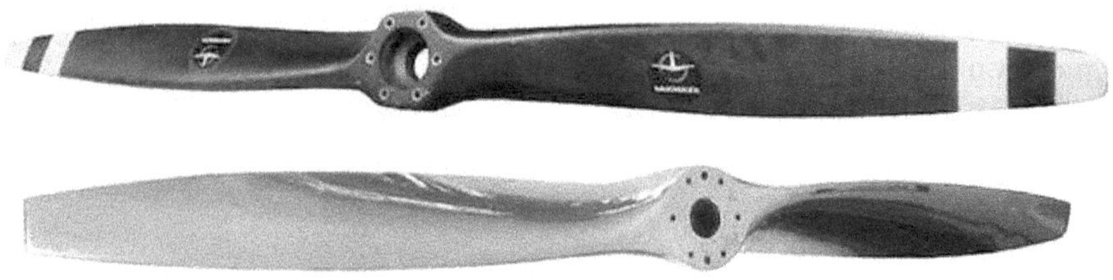

When it comes to more powerful engines, the propeller is larger to absorb the force developed by the engine. In these cases, a reduction mechanism or gearbox is typically installed between the engine output and the propeller, allowing the RPM of the propeller to differ from the RPM of the engine while maintaining values within optimal performance for aerodynamic efficiency.

Variable speed and variable pitch propellers

This type of propeller allows the pilot to adjust the pitch or blade angle. This means optimizing the relative angular position of the blades during different phases of flight, thereby achieving optimal performance at all times. The adjustment is made via the propeller pitch lever, which actuates a mechanism that can be mechanical, hydraulic, or electrical (see Figure 49). In some cases, this lever has only two positions: fine or short pitch (lower blade angle) and coarse or long pitch (higher blade angle), but it is more

common to select any pitch between a maximum and a minimum. To better understand the use of propeller pitch, it is important to consider the following two variables:

Most reciprocating engines generate their maximum power at a point close to maximum RPM.

The power required for economical flight at cruise speed is usually less than the maximum power the engine can produce.

Fine pitch implies a lower angle of attack of the blade; thus, it generates less induced drag. This combination allows the propeller to spin "more freely" and quickly, thereby achieving better utilization of engine power. Therefore, fine pitch is the most efficient angular position of the blades for maneuvers requiring maximum power: takeoff and climb. Fine pitch is not suitable for cruise conditions.

Coarse pitch assumes a higher angle of attack of the blades, resulting in greater induced drag. These variables require fewer RPM on the propeller, hence, a reduced engine power output. In this condition, it allows for the movement of a greater mass of air.

With this pitch, performance decreases during takeoff and climb; however, it increases efficiency at cruise speed, allowing the engine to operate at lower RPM and consume less fuel.

Constant speed and variable pitch propellers

This type of propeller combines the ability to vary blade pitch with an automated system. That is, the pitch is regulated automatically, maintaining a constant rotational speed of the propeller regardless of changes in engine power. These propellers have a governor that adjusts the blade pitch to maintain the revolutions selected by the pilot. This system allows for more efficient use of engine power at any flight regime. The use of variable-pitch propellers is also associated with larger aircraft. Fixed-pitch propellers equip engines of limited power; therefore, they are part of the propulsion systems of lightweight aircraft.

Propeller governor

More commonly known in aviation jargon as "governor," this is a system formed by an engine RPM detection device and a high-pressure oil pump. In a constant-speed propeller system, the governor responds to changes in engine RPM by directing pressurized oil to the hydraulic cylinder of the propeller or releasing oil from the hydraulic cylinder.

The change in oil volume within the hydraulic cylinder varies the blade angle and maintains the RPM of the propeller system. The governor can be set to a specific RPM value through the propeller control in the aircraft's cockpit.

In summary, the propeller governor compresses or releases the speed regulator spring, thereby controlling the angular movement of the propeller blades. Regarding flight operation and safety, it is important to recognize the main forces involved in controlling the pitch and operation of the propellers and governor, which are as follows:

Centrifugal Torque Moment: A centrifugal force vector acts on the blade and tends to reduce the selected pitch.

Governor Propellant Fluid Pressure: This force balances the counterweights of the blades; this system compensates for the force during the angular movement of pitch variation.

Feedback Springs: The governor assembly is subjected to mechanical load through the springs. These springs generate opposing force to the fluid thrust, balancing the control forces of the blades' angular movement.

Aerodynamic Torque Forces: The aerodynamic effect generates forces that tend to rotate the blade to the maximum pitch or fine pitch position; the rest of the system and acting forces compensate for these loads and maintain the blade in equilibrium.

Propeller synchronization: Most multi-engine aircraft are equipped with propeller synchronization systems. These systems provide a means to control and synchronize the RPM of the engines. Through synchronization, vibrations are reduced, and the unpleasant movement and sound produced by unsynchronized propeller operation are eliminated.

The principle of operation of this system is based on an electrical device that measures the RPM produced by both engines and makes the necessary corrections to ensure they deliver the same number of revolutions. Similarly, it establishes a relationship between the operation of both propellers, aiming to create a single phase of operation that reduces vibrations and annoying noise.

The control mechanism is located in the cockpit, usually alongside the engine controls. In the vast majority of aircraft equipped with this technology, the synchronization system also has control over the governor and the angular movement or pitch of the propellers, ensuring that synchronization is comprehensive and truly optimizes the operation of both propulsion systems.

Biblioteca
Aeronáutica
aviación en simples pasos

Chapter 4

Engines

Biblioteca
Aeronáutica
aviación en simples pasos

Engine components

To better understand the operation and primary components of the opposed-cylinder engine, we will use a real-world example. Thus, the description will refer to the Avco Lycoming O-360, which is one of the most commonly used engines in light aircraft such as the Cessna 172, Cessna 177, Piper PA-28, Piper PA-24, Mooney M-20, Aero Boero 180, among others.

Main Mechanical Components

The engine we are referencing is a four-cylinder opposed, normally aspirated engine with a carburetor. With the help of the Lycoming Illustrated Parts Catalog, we will proceed with the description and operation of each primary component. It is crucial to note that an engine is a complex assembly where all parts must function in coordination to generate the necessary power and RPM.

We will then focus on the auxiliary systems and components that contribute to the overall engine function. In the following diagram, you can observe the overhead view of the assembled Lycoming O-360 engine, without accessories. Let's examine the main parts.

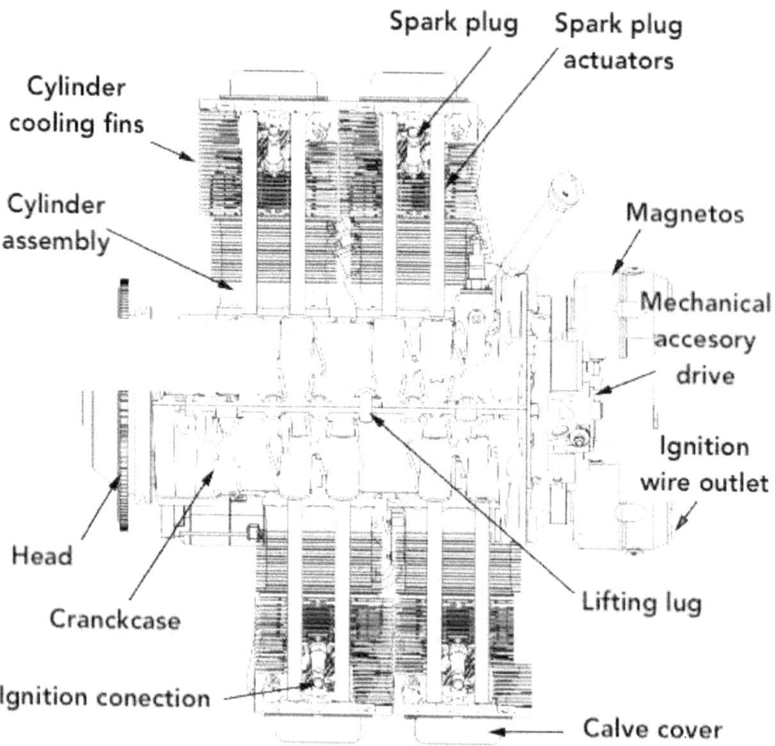

In the previous figure, you can see the engine block assembly, with installed cylinders, the outer valve guides, spark plug connections and ignition harness, magneto coils, and the mechanical transmission assembly.

The structure containing all components and where all physical and chemical processes occur is the pair of half-blocks and the cylinders; in the case of the described engine, there are four cylinders.

Both half-blocks, when joined, encase the crankshaft and camshaft inside. These two fundamental shafts of the engine are mechanically isolated by bearings. Bearings are hardened steel seats that support the crankshaft and camshaft bearings; each is lubricated to prevent "metal-to-metal" contact. Bearings are located in the block bearing areas.

The half-blocks are cast (either alpha iron or ductile steel), and each component is pre-formed with its respective housing, inserts, and mounting systems. The joining of both half-blocks is achieved through internal bolts (commonly known as "studs") and external anchor bolts. Contact surfaces are protected and sealed with gaskets, spacers, and silicone seals. The joined half-blocks are referred to as the engine block.

The engine block functions as a sealed and continuously lubricated mechanical unit. A failure in the lubrication system can lead to a sudden collapse of any of the main components; we will discuss common issues later.

The ends of the block are also closed, with connections at the rear to the gear train and accessories and at the front with the main seal for the crankshaft flange (facing the propeller installation). As a horizontally opposed engine, these assemblies are installed on the sides of each half-block and become part of the closed and lubricated system.

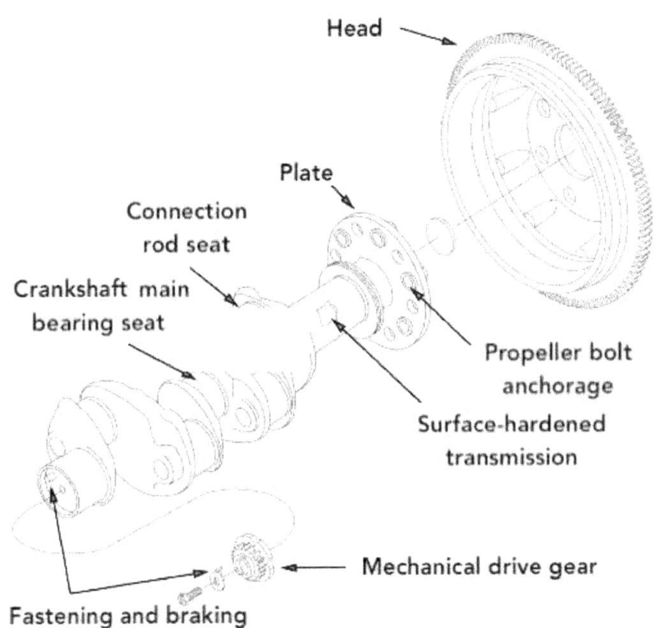

In this figure, the crankshaft configuration is depicted. It is the main shaft of the engine, directly linking the motion of each connecting rod within the cylinders and transmitting angular velocity to the propeller, which is mounted on its end or flange. At the opposite end, a gear is installed that transmits work and angular velocity to the engine accessories, camshaft, and other components (oil pump, fuel pump, vacuum pump, among others).

Crankshafts are manufactured from a highly resistant steel alloy (a uniform medium-grain tempered martensite solid solution), and surface hardening treatments are applied to enhance resistance to surface and subsurface cracking as well as corrosive processes.

For several years, it has been mandatory for all crankshafts to undergo a vacuum arc reheat treatment (VAR). Airworthiness directives exist regarding this requirement, which both owners and maintenance personnel must verify to maintain the engine's airworthy condition.

The construction materials and treatments applied ensure that the crankshaft maintains safe operating characteristics while retaining the necessary flexibility during each engine cycle, as well as the capacity to transmit and absorb the high workload stresses produced.

Although not the case here, it is worth mentioning that larger engine models may feature internal counterweights on their crankshafts to balance their operation.

In the following figure, the camshaft is shown at the top of the diagram. This component is the second main shaft of the engine. Like the crankshaft, its supports in the block are controlled by hardened metals which, along with the lubricant, prevent wear. The camshaft rotates due to the angular motion transmitted by the gears connecting it to the crankshaft; its function is to sequentially generate the impulse for opening and closing the intake and exhaust valves in each of the cylinders.

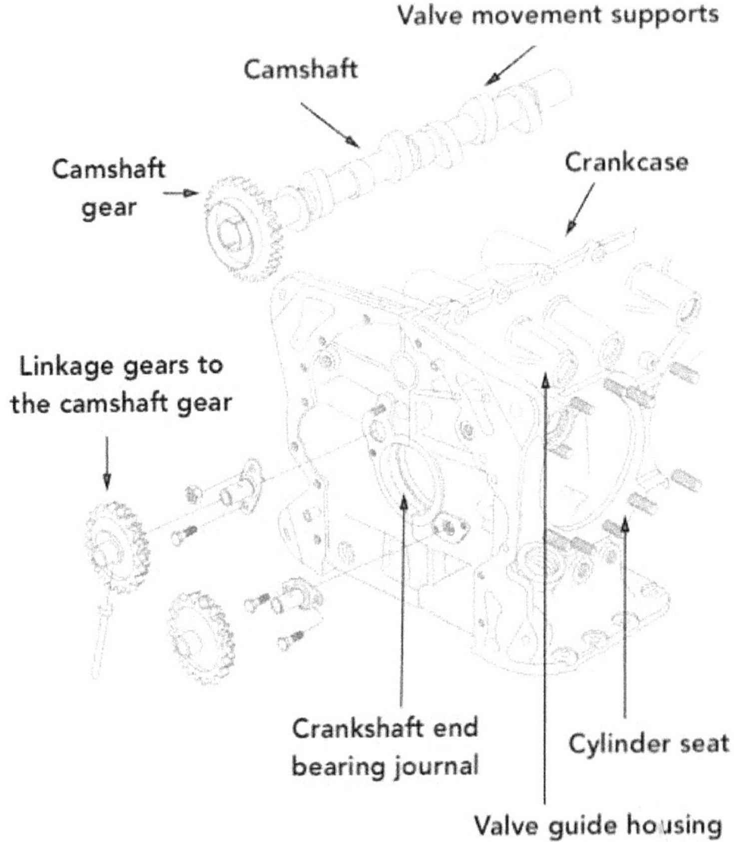

The sequence of opening and closing the intake and exhaust valves is crucial for the Otto Cycle to proceed with the expected performance, thus achieving the necessary power output from the engine. The four cylinder assemblies are located on the sides of the block, as explained in the previous paragraphs. Likewise, the connecting rod-piston assemblies are also fixed and positioned to the sides within each cylinder. This forms a sealed chamber where the thermodynamic processes we have discussed occur.

An important feature to highlight is that the contact surfaces of both the crankshaft and camshaft are mirror-polished. The aim of this is to enhance synergy with the lubricant to prevent metal-to-metal contact. In the following image, we can see a crankshaft undergoing its inspection process, dimensional control, and polishing of the contact surfaces.

In the previous image, we can observe a four-cylinder crankshaft undergoing a major inspection. These tasks include material grinding, dimensional control, non-destructive testing (verification of surface and internal damage using magnetizable particles and other tests), and polishing of the aforementioned surfaces. In the following diagram, we can see how the piston assembly of the cylinder is configured.

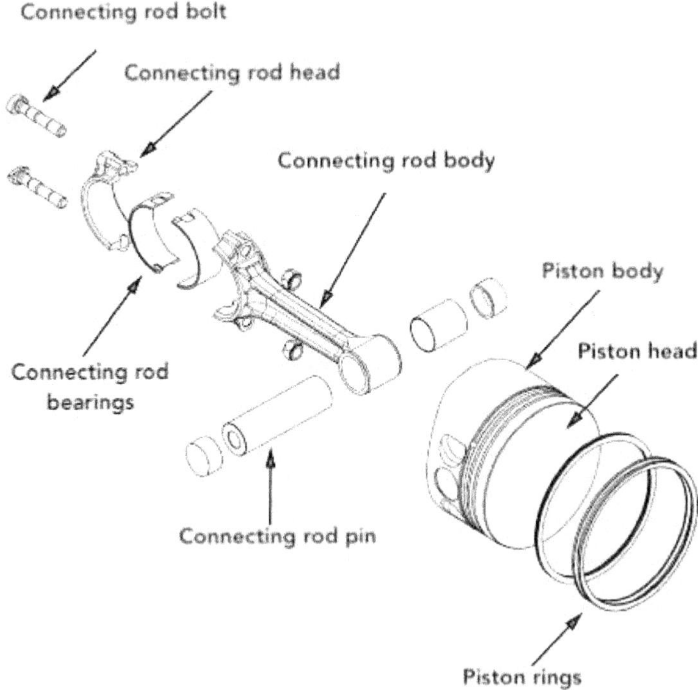

As seen in the previous figure, the connecting rod is a reinforced steel arm, with one end featuring the housing and bushing for the pin that links to the piston; while the opposite end has the connecting rod head where the bearings are located. This end is the attachment point with the crankshaft.

The piston is attached to the connecting rod by the internal pin, allowing necessary freedom of movement during the piston's up-and-down stroke within the cylinder. The piston is manufactured from an extremely durable aluminum alloy and is forged.

The piston body is equipped with a set of rings around its circumference, serving a dual purpose: on one hand, they seal the space between the internal cylinder wall and the piston body, and on the other hand, they facilitate piston movement by acting as lubricated guides. Additionally, behind the set of rings is a final ring whose sole function is to retain the lubricant.

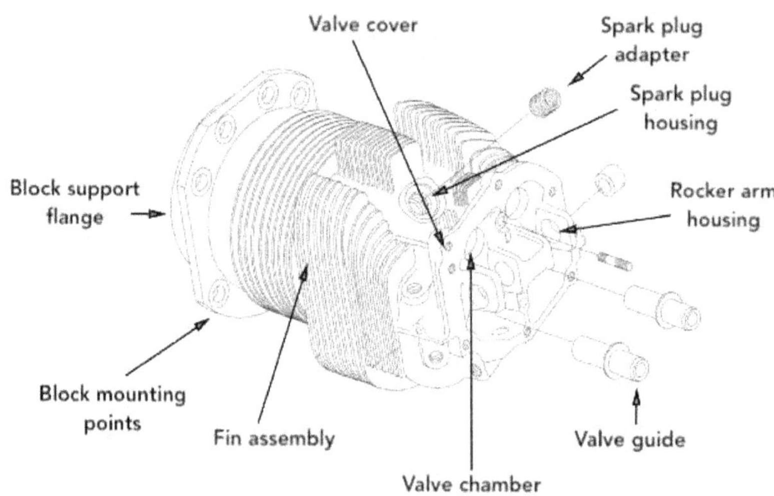

The piston rings are manufactured from particularly hard steel alloys to prevent wear effects under high temperatures. The piston crown, in turn, undergoes specific treatments to enhance its resistance to high temperatures and the substantial loads produced during combustion.

The cylinder head, along with the rings and the internal cylinder body, forms the sealed chamber where combustion occurs.

In the cylinder shown, we can observe the main components. The exterior wall is covered with cooling fins designed to dissipate heat from the inside of the component to the outside; the impact air action provides the necessary cooling to keep the engine operation within safe ranges. The base of the cylinder features a lip that fits into the block connection, and the block's anchored bolts are seated in the base's holes.

Regardless of the specific engine being analyzed, it's crucial to recognize the critical nature of the cylinder assembly in engine operation. The block, crankshaft, and camshaft are highly reliable and robust due to their materials and function; however, with respect to the cylinders, we must always understand that:

1. The assembly structure must be sufficiently strong to withstand the combustion loads.

2. The construction material must have heat dissipation capability and be lightweight.

3. All moving parts must be perfectly calibrated, adjusted, lubricated, and installed. Any adjustment or securing discrepancies can lead to critical mechanical failure.

At the top of the cylinder, valves are installed over the intake and exhaust ports. Above them and their springs, the rocker arms are positioned, which pivot on an axis mounted to the cylinder body. The upper structure features threaded holes where the fuel feeder is attached, allowing fuel to enter the chamber.

In the following figure, the cylinder valve assembly is depicted. Each valve is installed within the cylinder and compressed by two springs (some engines may use three). These springs are supported by tappets. The forced opening and closing of the valves, controlled by the rocker arms and springs, allow for the sealing of the cylinder chamber and alternate the intake and exhaust processes.

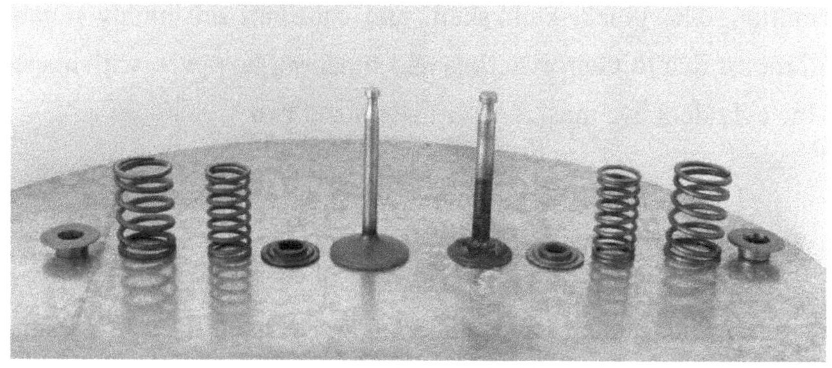

The rocker arms transmit the lifting force from the camshaft to the valves. The rocker arm supports are mounted on plain, roller, or ball bearings, or a combination thereof, which serve as pivots. Typically, one end of the rocker arm presses against the pushrod, while the other end interfaces with the valve stem. The rocker arm end generally includes an adjustment screw to set the clearance between the rocker arm and the valve stem tip.

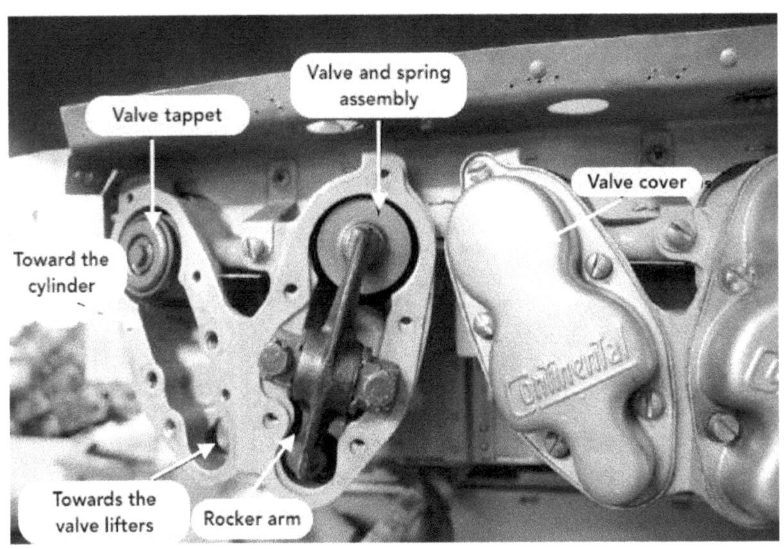

In the previous image, the installation of the valve and spring assembly in the intake and exhaust positions of the cylinder can be observed. In this case, the lateral separated arrangement corresponds to a larger capacity cylinder, such as the one in the Teledyne Continental TSIO-540 engine.

On the side of the cylinder, there is a threaded hole for the spark plug. The graphic also shows an adapter insert, used in cases of re-machining and to allow the use of standard-size spark plugs.

The electrical connection to the spark plugs is routed through the ignition harness or wiring. In subsequent chapters, we will delve deeper into the ignition system; for now, we are merely referencing the installation. The following image illustrates the installation of the magneto coils, the ignition harness, and one of the spark plugs as an example.

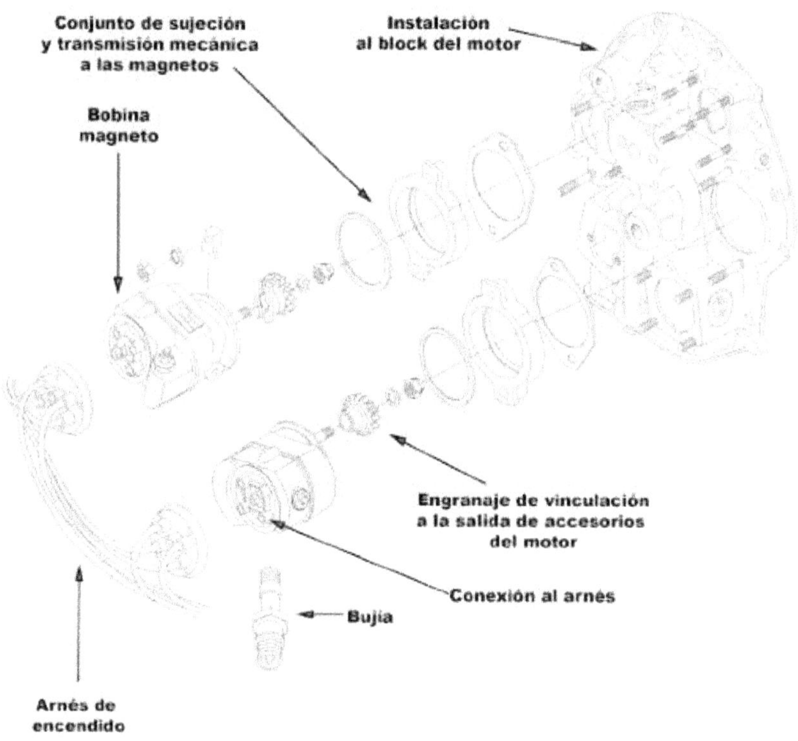

All aircraft engines are equipped with a dual ignition system to ensure reliability. The certification standards are FAR 33 (U.S. Federal Aviation Regulations for Aircraft Engines) and JAR 33 (for the European Union). Other countries have aligned their certification standards with these regulations.

In the next figure, both magnetos are installed and mounted at the rear of the engine accessories. From both devices, the wiring harness leads to the spark plugs. The operation of the magnetos and spark plugs will be detailed later when we focus on engine ignition.

The rear accessory section is part of the engine block, made of cast iron, and houses the various gear trains that drive the magnetos and system pumps. The gear trains consist of straight and bevel gears, and the entire assembly is contained in a sealed and lubricated chamber, similar to the other mechanical components of the block and cylinders.

Behind the engine, we also observe the engine mounting assembly to the aircraft structure, known as the engine mount or "bancada." The mount is a structural support made of steel tubes (typically AISI 4130 steel). Between the mount and the engine itself is the fire shield, a steel sheet covering that isolates the engine and fuel system from the rest of the aircraft. The structural assembly will be described in detail in subsequent paragraphs.

In the preceding paragraphs, we described the main mechanical components of the O-360 engine. Additionally, we need to consider the following auxiliary systems and essential accessory components for the engine's complete functionality:

Ignition System: Composed of the coils, magnetos, ignition wiring or harness, and spark plugs. We will explore the specifics of each component of this system in the following paragraphs.

Lubrication System: Consists of the mechanical oil pump, internal block ducts, and other distribution piping. Oil flows under pressure through the ducts to the lubrication ports of the block, crankshaft, bearings, and camshaft. The pump generates the necessary pressure to maintain a lubricating film separating all the engine's metal components.

It is important to mention that a partial obstruction in the lubrication ducts within the block or bearings, during cruise power operation, will cause a critical mechanical failure in less than 5 seconds of operation. Lack of lubrication in the main components results in metal-to-metal contact, which rapidly leads to crankshaft fracture or rod detachment. These are the most common failures originating from lubrication issues.

Ignition system

The ignition system of a reciprocating engine comprises a combination of electrical and mechanical devices whose primary function is to provide a constant spark while the engine is operating. To understand its operation, it's crucial to first differentiate between the two types of ignition systems: those using magneto coils and those equipped with Full Authority Digital Engine Control (FADEC) systems.

Magneto Ignition System

In a separate chapter, we will cover concepts related to onboard electrical power generation. For now, we'll focus on the fundamentals and main components of engines equipped with magnetos:

- Magneto Coils
- Starter Motor
- Ignition Harness
- Spark Plugs

Magneto ignition systems can be further classified into high-tension or low-tension systems. The low-tension magneto system generates a lower voltage which is distributed to a transformer coil located near each spark plug. This system mitigates some issues inherent in the high-tension system, which transmitted high voltage directly through the spark plug. Previously, ignition cables could not withstand the high voltage and were prone to leaking to ground before the spark reached the cylinder. Advances in materials and shielding have resolved these issues, making the high-tension magneto system the most commonly used ignition system in aircraft.

Magneto Coils: These consist of a basic alternating current generator that receives mechanical impulse from the engine's gear train. Like any generator, its function is to convert mechanical energy into electrical energy, utilizing principles of electromagnetism through a permanent magnet and a traditional wound coil.

As electrical energy is generated, it is transmitted through the ignition harness or wiring to each of the spark plugs installed in the cylinders. Within the magneto, at the correct moment, the current flow stops, and the magnetic field collapses through a second set of windings in the coil, generating a high voltage. This voltage is used to bridge the gap of the spark plug. In both cases, the three basic components necessary for generating electrical energy are present to develop the high voltage that forces a spark to jump across the gap of the spark plug in each cylinder.

The operation of the magneto is synchronized with the engine so that a spark occurs only when the piston is at the appropriate stroke at a specific number of degrees of crankshaft rotation before the piston reaches top dead center (TDC).

There are both single magnetos and dual magnetos, which can be used interchangeably in aircraft engines. The design of a single magneto incorporates the distributor within the housing along with the magneto switch assembly, a rotating magnet, and the coil;

these three components produce the electromagnetic effect for generating electricity. The dual magneto incorporates two magnetos contained within a single housing or structure. The dual magneto coil consists of a rotating magnet and a cam that are common to two sets of breaker points and coils.

Ignition Sequence

The synchronization of the magnetos is vital for the overall proper functioning of the system. While there is a tolerance margin (regarding time and position), it is necessary to maintain its tuning within the established tolerance values. The relationship between ignition timing synchronization and the energy transmitted depends on the number of engine cylinders and the internal volume of the chamber. This synchronization process is known as the firing order.

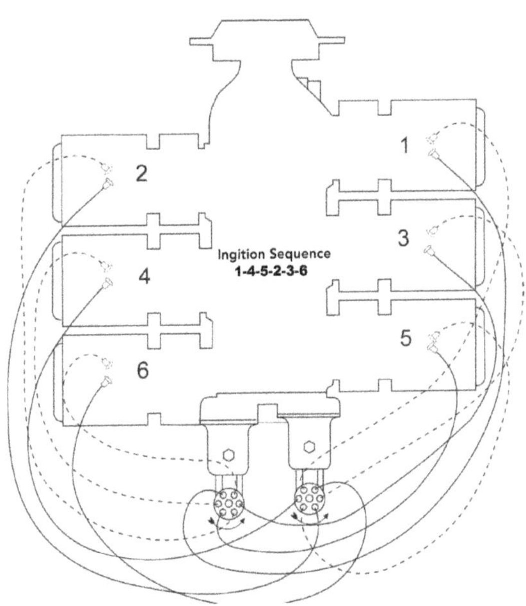

In the previous figure, we observe the firing order of a Lycoming IO-540 engine. Like all aircraft engines, it is equipped with two magneto coils. From each coil, a wire connects it to each of the cylinders, thus, each cylinder receives two wires that independently energize each spark plug. This is commonly known as a dual ignition system.

In the previous figure, we can see the connection details and the ignition method of the engine, known as the firing order. This defines the chronological order in which combustion occurs in each of the cylinders. As mentioned at the outset, the four strokes of the Otto Cycle develop in the cylinders in a specific working order.

It should be noted that different reciprocating engine manufacturers number the cylinders differently; therefore, the firing sequence will vary, for example, between Avco Lycoming engines and Teledyne Continental engines.

The electrical impulse from the magnetos must be perfectly synchronized so that both coils energize the spark plug simultaneously. This ensures complete combustion of the air-fuel mixture introduced into the cylinder chamber. To ensure this description is clear not only in theory but also as a flight operation safety element, it is important to always consider the following variables:

- Condition of the ignition wiring harness and insulation
- Condition of the connections
- Synchronization of the magnetos

Operation of the reciprocating engine

Most reciprocating engines operate based on the principle of the four-stroke Otto cycle. The Otto cycle is a thermodynamic cycle that describes the physical principle of operation of internal combustion engines (reciprocating or rotary in aviation). This cycle was discovered in 1876 by the German engineer Nicolaus Otto (1832-1891), who later applied it in the invention of the first internal combustion engine.

This thermodynamic principle governs both two-stroke and four-stroke internal combustion engines; four-stroke engines include diesel engines. For the purposes of this book, we will focus on the four-stroke cycle, which is used by aviation reciprocating engines.

The Otto Cycle for four-stroke engines consists of four stages or strokes: intake, compression, combustion, and exhaust. The following diagram illustrates how these four strokes occur within the cylinder, piston, and crankshaft assembly.

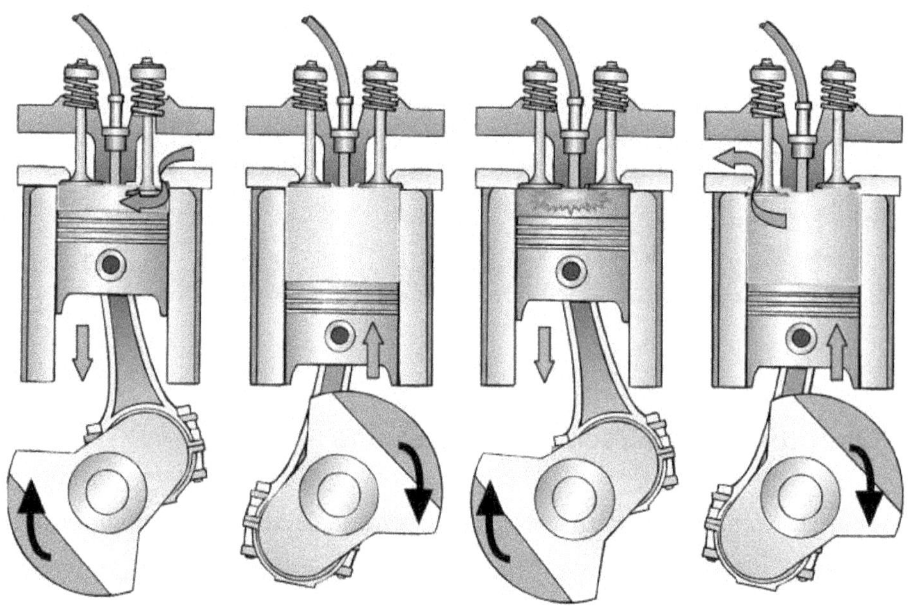

The four strokes observed in the previous figure encompass the sequential process that occurs within each cylinder of the engine. The work generated by each piston drives the crankshaft, which subsequently rotates the propeller, thereby creating the aerodynamic effect that provides the final propulsion for the aircraft. Let's delve into how this phenomenon occurs in detail.

The principle of the engine's four strokes occurs in a single revolution or RPM. In other words, during one complete rotation of the crankshaft, the following four steps take place:

Intake

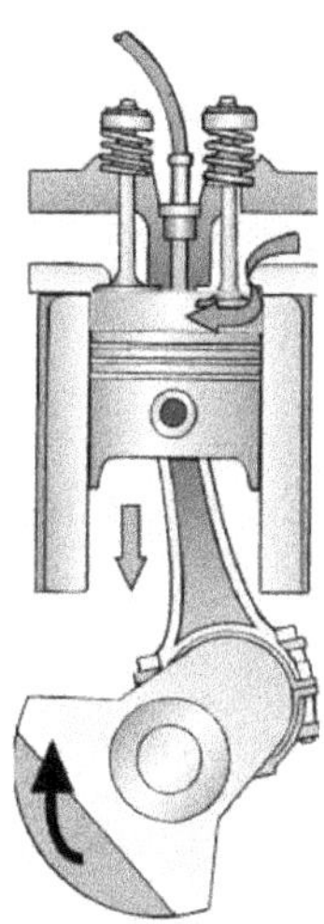

When the intake valve of the cylinder opens, while the exhaust valve remains closed, a mass of air enters the cylinder chamber. This phenomenon is due to the suction effect created by the piston during its downward stroke towards bottom dead center. The piston acts like a plunger that draws in air during this stroke. By the time the connecting rod and piston reach bottom dead center, the necessary amount of air for combustion has entered the cylinder.

The downward movement of the piston is driven by the connecting rod, which is integral with the crankshaft. The crankshaft is precisely responsible for coordinating the movement of all connecting rods and pistons within each cylinder in a sequential and harmonized manner.

Compression

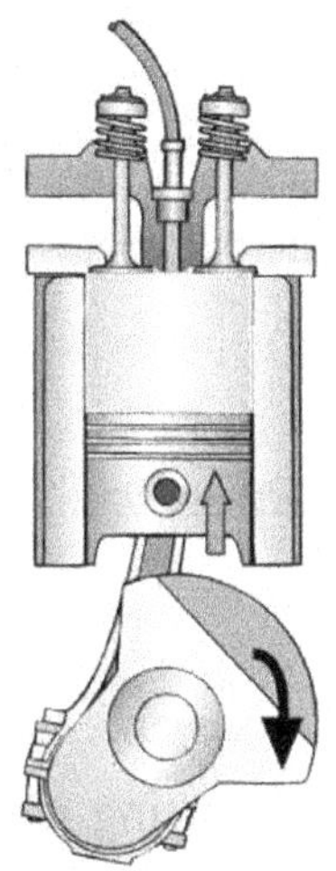

After reaching bottom dead center, the connecting rod and piston begin their upward stroke towards top dead center. When the piston reaches bottom dead center, the intake valve closes, creating a sealed chamber within the cylinder. A medida que avanza el recorrido del pistón sobre las paredes del cilindro, el aire contenido se comprime.

As the piston travels upwards along the cylinder walls, the contained air is compressed.

When the piston reaches top dead center, the air mass is at its maximum compression. The connecting rod and piston maintain this position for a fraction of a second until the next phase begins.

Combustion

With the cylinder chamber filled with compressed air and both valves closed, fuel enters and then the spark plug ignites. The spark from the spark plug causes the vaporized fuel, along with the air mass inside the cylinder, to ignite suddenly, resulting in a controlled explosion. The combustion of the fuel, like any explosion, releases a significant amount of energy in the form of heat and pressure. The sudden increase in pressure in the chamber drives the piston (piston and connecting rod assembly) towards bottom dead center, marking the beginning of the fourth stage of the cycle. Once combustion occurs, the exhaust valve opens to allow the combustion by-products to exit through the exhaust.

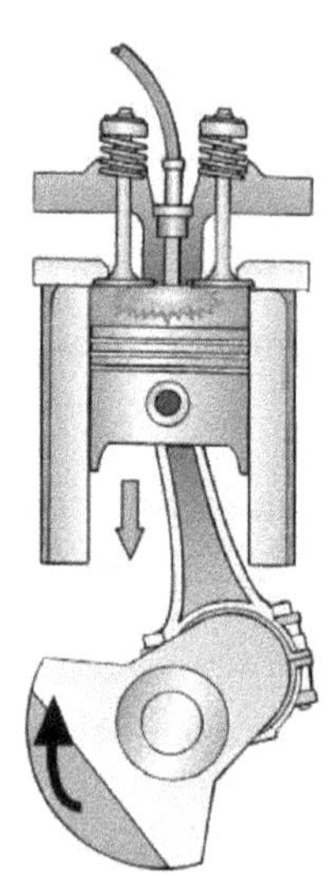

Expansion

The pressure contained in the chamber after combustion causes an expansion effect that literally pushes the piston (piston and connecting rod assembly) towards top dead center. The energy from the expansion of combustion is converted into mechanical work that is transmitted through the connecting rod to the crankshaft. With the exhaust valve closed during the final phase of expansion, the intake valve opens again to initiate the intake stroke of the next cycle.

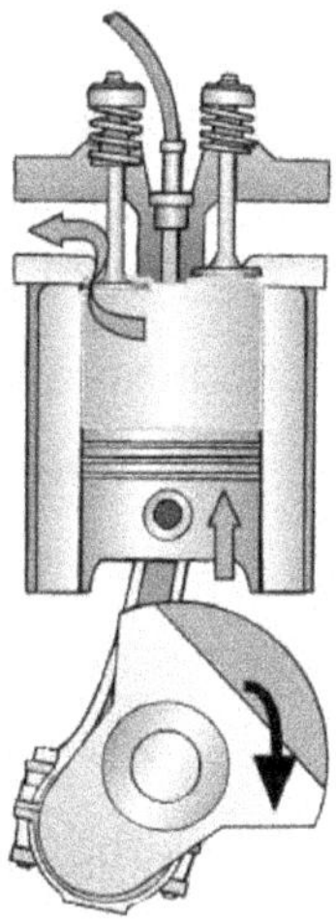

The four strokes described in the preceding paragraphs occur sequentially in each cylinder of the engine. The mechanical work transmitted to the crankshaft by each cylinder assembly determines the force and speed at which the crankshaft rotates. In other words, the energy produced by each cylinder assembly and the sequence of the process translate into revolutions per minute (RPM) and horsepower (hp) or kilowatts (kW).

The Otto Cycle, in theory, is an ideal adiabatic thermodynamic cycle. However, in practice, the transformations occurring in the cylinder chamber do not occur at constant volume. Therefore, the Otto Cycle remains a theoretical expression serving as the foundation for the physical principle governing internal combustion engines.

The efficiency of the engine depends on the compression ratio. This ratio represents the maximum volume available in the sealed cylinder chamber, delimited between top dead center and bottom dead center. The compression ratio dictates the type of gasoline (octane rating) required to optimize the energy from combustion expansion. In aviation engines, fuel use is limited to

AVGAS 100 LL; later, we will discuss the specifics of this low-lead aviation fuel.

Additionally, the ratio between air mass and fuel that generates the explosion must be considered. This ratio is known as the "mixture ratio." We will delve into this concept later. For now, it's important to note that the mixture is a specific ratio of air and fuel that results in a controlled energy release explosion. In chemistry, this air-fuel ratio is referred to as the stoichiometric ratio, which defines the conditions where each constituent element is present in a specific amount to achieve the desired reaction—in this case, a controlled exothermic reaction of temperature and pressure.

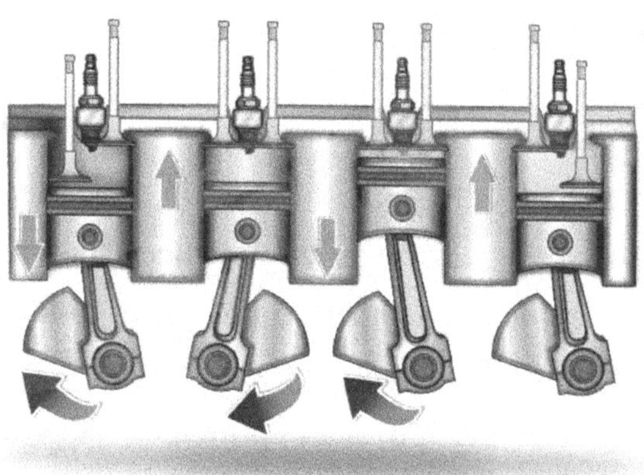

Before diving into the detailed operation, mechanics, and specifics of opposed-cylinder engines, it is necessary to review some fundamental theoretical concepts to better understand the subsequent content. Below, we summarize the essential knowledge needed for a thorough grasp of each concept.

What is Mechanical Work?

The fundamentals of engineering and continuous mechanics state that work is the force that alters the state of motion of a body. Formally, work is defined as the force exerted on a body that equals the amount of energy required to move it in an accelerated manner. Work is expressed as a scalar physical quantity with the unit of reference being the Joule. In colloquial terms, work can be described as the force that changes or provides the necessary movement to a mechanical system or assembly.

What is power?

Power is the rate at which mechanical work is performed over time. The concept can also be associated with the speed of energy change within the same system needed to accomplish a certain amount of mechanical work. Analytically, it can be expressed as the total energy of a system divided by time or time unit.

What is horsepower?

As explained earlier, horsepower represents the amount of mechanical work the engine develops to produce power. While this definition is accurate, it is theoretical. There are factors that reduce power output, with friction being the most significant. Even though components are lubricated and well-coordinated, friction between components reduces the final power output. The actual power output of an engine is commonly referred to as “horsepower."

What is Compression in the Engine?

The compression ratio of an opposed-cylinder engine quantifies the volume where the air-fuel mixture is compressed before combustion within the cylinder chamber. In other words, it is the maximum volume the compressed mixture can occupy within the sealed cylinder chamber.

The compression ratio defines the thermal performance of the entire engine assembly. This variable indicates the level of efficiency in utilizing the fuel's energy, transformed into thermal energy and subsequently into mechanical energy. The compression ratio of an opposed-cylinder engine varies depending on the required RPM.

What is Fuel Octane Rating?

The octane number or octane rating is a dimensionless scale that quantifies the anti-detonant capability of refined hydrocarbons in gasoline when compressed within the cylinder chamber. This quality allows the fuel to ignite when the spark plug fires, generating combustion. Generally, engine efficiency increases with the octane rating, as this condition is controlled mainly by the anti-detonant capacity of the fuel used.

In essence, the octane number provides qualitative information about the fuel's response in combustion and the energy it will release at that instance. The text will later delve into fuel characteristics, octane ratings, and other important details.

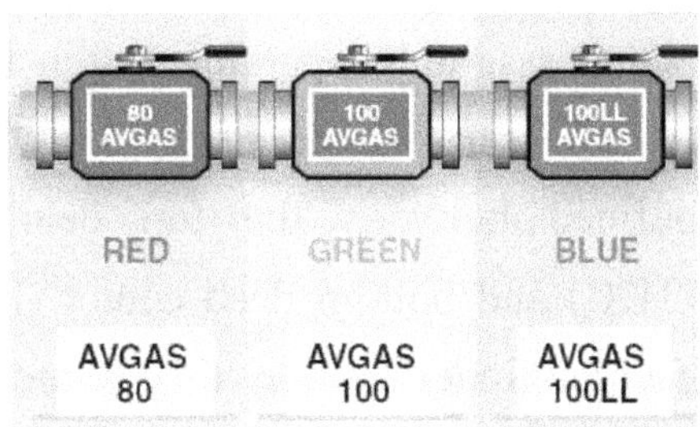

What are RPM?

RPM stands for "revolutions per minute," which is a bit obvious, right? But what do engine RPMs represent? RPMs are an expression of angular velocity, quantifying the number of rotations of a body per minute. Typically, this "body" in question is a shaft linked to some mechanical system.

In the case of the opposed-cylinder engine, the key shaft is the crankshaft, as it is the primary component linking the movement of each connecting rod-piston assembly within the cylinders, and it transmits angular movement and force to the propeller. Thus, the reference for rotation measurement is the crankshaft.

What is Displacement?

Displacement is the sum of the total useful volume of the cylinder chambers. It is usually expressed in cubic centimeters (cc) or cubic inches, representing the area where the connecting rod-piston assembly operates within the Otto Cycle. The volume of each cylinder is defined between the top dead center (TDC) and bottom dead center (BDC) of each cylinder. While this expression is predominantly applied to inline engines, some aviation engines also use this characterization in their specifications.

What is Engine Efficiency?

The aviation opposed-cylinder engine's efficiency is expressed in three ways: mechanical efficiency, thermal efficiency, and overall engine efficiency. Mechanical efficiency is the measure of the actual power an engine can generate and thus be utilized by the propeller assembly. In aviation engines, mechanical efficiency typically ranges from 85% to 90%. Thermal efficiency represents the amount of heat converted into mechanical work based on the combustion and expansion process. The total engine efficiency is the ratio between the actual power obtained and the energy produced to generate that power.

Operation of the Jet engines

In contrast to what was discussed in the previous paragraphs, we will outline the general principles of the thermodynamic cycle utilized by jet engines, based on a principle known as the Brayton cycle.

The Brayton cycle, or Joule cycle or Froude cycle, is the thermodynamic principle of a compressible fluid (air) that consists of a compression stage, a heating stage, and an adiabatic expansion. This simple principle forms the basis for countless industrial processes and, above all, is the fundamental theoretical basis of the jet engine.The application of gas turbine technology based on the Brayton cycle to air propulsion is attributed to the English engineer Frank Whittle, who patented the idea in 1927 and proposed it to the British Air Force.

A series of experts led by Alan Arnold Griffith had studied the technical possibilities of the gas turbine as a means of air propulsion in the preceding years, although their idea was based on using the mechanical work obtained to drive a propeller. Whittle, on the other hand, proposed a Brayton cycle that would not produce any net mechanical work, so that the turbine would generate just enough energy to drive the compressor.

The propulsion, according to him, would be due to the high velocity of the gases exiting the turbine, forming a propulsive jet that would generate thrust on the engine.

In this image, you can see the schematic of a turbojet engine (such as the Pratt Whitney JT3) without bypass flow. The arrows indicate the mass of air entering and undergoing compression in different stages. When the compressed mass reaches the combustion chambers, it mixes with fuel and undergoes combustion, characterized not by explosion but by a high release of pressure and temperature.

The energy released drives the turbine stages and expands through the engine's exhaust nozzle, generating thrust force. The non-explosive combustion is due to the use of high-performance fuels with high octane (or detonation) ratings. In the current aviation industry, the use of JET A-1 is standardized for such engines. JET A-1 is a refined kerosene byproduct with high energy-generating capacity and anti-detonation additives.

In this type of engine, the aircraft's propulsion capability is expressed in terms of thrust in kilograms-force (kgf), rather than horsepower (hp).

Chapter 5

Fuel

AVGAS/ Aviation Fuel

Biblioteca
Aeronáutica
aviación en simples pasos

Introduction

The specification of an ideal fuel for a turbine engine or a piston engine would include the following key requirements:

- Easy flow in all operating conditions.
- Complete combustion under all conditions.
- High calorific value.
- Non-corrosive.
- Low fire risk.
- Ease of engine starting.
- Lubrication.

Piston engine fuel

Aircraft with piston engines use gasoline-based fuels grouped under the title AVGAS (aviation gasoline). To ensure aviation gasoline meets the above requirements, it is manufactured to stringent "specifications" issued by the Engine Research and Development Directorate (DERD).

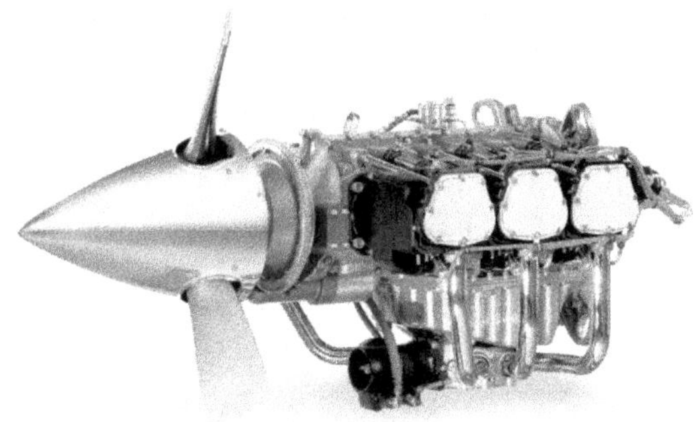

The octane rating of the fuel is specified by grade, e.g., AVGAS 100 is a 100-octane fuel. Higher-octane fuels are used in high-performance engines with high compression ratios. The most popular grades of AVGAS available today are:

AVGAS/ Aviation Fuel

Grade	Performance No.	Colour	Specific Gravity (Density)	
AVGAS 100LL	100/130	Blue	0.72	Low Lead
AVGAS 100	100/130	Green	0.72	High Lead
AVGAS 115	115/145	Green	0.72	High Lead

Jet engine fuel

Aircraft with turbine engines use kerosene-based fuels. The two main types of turbine fuel commonly used in civil aircraft are shown below, along with their characteristic properties:

AVTUR (Aviation turbine fuel)

JET A1. This is a kerosene-type fuel with a nominal SG of 0.8 at 15 °C. It has a flash point of 38 °C and a freezing point of -47 °C.

JET A is a similar type of fuel with the same SG and flash point, but it has a freezing point of -40 °C.

AVTAG (Aviation turbine gasoline)

JET B. This is a wide-cut gasoline/kerosene blend fuel with a nominal SG of 0.77 at 15 °C. It has a flash point as low as -20 °C, a wider boiling range than JET A1, and a freezing point of -60 °C. JET B can be used as an alternative to JET A1.

Turbine fuels are not dyed for identification purposes; they retain their natural color, which can range from a dull yellow to completely colorless. If a fuel sample appears cloudy, there could be several reasons. If the irregularity seems to rise rapidly to the top of the sample, air is present. If the irregularity settles slowly to the bottom of the sample, water is present in the fuel. A cloudy appearance typically indicates the presence of water.

Water is always present in fuel, and the quantity will vary depending on the manufacturer's quality control efficiency and preventive measures taken during storage and transfer. New measures can be taken to minimize water accumulation once the fuel has been transferred to the aircraft's tanks:

Water Drainage: If fuel can settle after refueling, water droplets, which are heavier than fuel, will sink to the bottom of the tank and can then be drained through the water drain valve.

Fuel Heater: A fuel heater is provided in turbine engine fuel systems to prevent water from freezing and blocking fuel filters.

In gas turbine engine systems, fuel passes through a heat exchanger using hot compressor supply air to remove any ice crystals that may have formed while the fuel was exposed to the extremely low temperatures experienced at high altitudes. Some systems also use a fuel-cooled oil cooler, which utilizes hot engine oil to heat the fuel and, in turn, cools the oil.

Internal Atmosphere: Once the fuel is in the aircraft's fuel tanks, the main source of water contamination is the atmosphere that remains inside the tank. If the tanks are filled, the atmosphere and the moisture it contains are excluded, thus minimizing the likelihood of fuel contamination.

Fuel system

Fuel is stored and transported within the aircraft in tanks that can be integral, rigid, or flexible.

Integral Tanks: Located within the wings and, depending on the type, the center section's torsion box and the horizontal stabilizer. These are sealed during manufacturing to provide large-volume fuel storage. The advantage of this tank type is that little extra weight is added to the aircraft since the tank structure is formed by the already-required aircraft structure. Used in commercial aircraft.

Rigid Tank: A sealed metal container mounted in the aircraft's wing or fuselage. Simple, but adds extra weight and requires a mounting structure. More popular in light aircraft. This type of tank can be externally installed, such as on the wingtip, made of metal or composite construction.

Flexible Tank: Bags made of sealed rubberized fabric, sometimes referred to as fuel bladders or bag tanks. This type of tank requires a structure within the aircraft to hold and support it. They are typically mounted inside the wing or fuselage and are more popular in military aircraft, as they can be effectively "self-sealing" in the event of battle damage.

Baffles are placed inside the tank to minimize large inertial forces generated when the fuel surges during aircraft maneuvers, acceleration, deceleration, or side slipping, for example. Some large aircraft may be equipped with baffle check valves that allow fuel to flow inboard but not outboard toward the wingtips during maneuvers. Fuel tanks also incorporate vents, water drains, feed pipes, measurement systems, and filler caps. In larger aircraft, tanks will also have boost pumps, high- and low-level float switches, pressure refueling valves, and filters.

The aircraft's fuel system is designed to store and deliver fuel to the engine system. It must be capable of supplying more fuel than the engine can use during its most critical flight phase to ensure the engine never runs out of fuel.

In a simple and light aircraft fuel system, fuel tanks are usually rigid tanks mounted in the wings and filled by the "overwing" method (open line through a filler cap on top of the tank). These aircraft can use a gravity-feed system or a pressure-pump system.

For example, the fuel system of a **Cessna 172** is discussed. It offers two metal fuel tanks with a capacity of 13 gallons each. These tanks are located above the wings.

From the tanks, the fuel travels through hoses or lines to a **shut-off valve**, which either permits or restricts the flow to the engine. It then continues its journey to the **primer** injector before completing its path to the engine and the carburetor. It is of utmost importance to understand the fuel's path within the system in order to comprehend how it feeds the engine. Below is a diagram representing this system to better understand its flow:

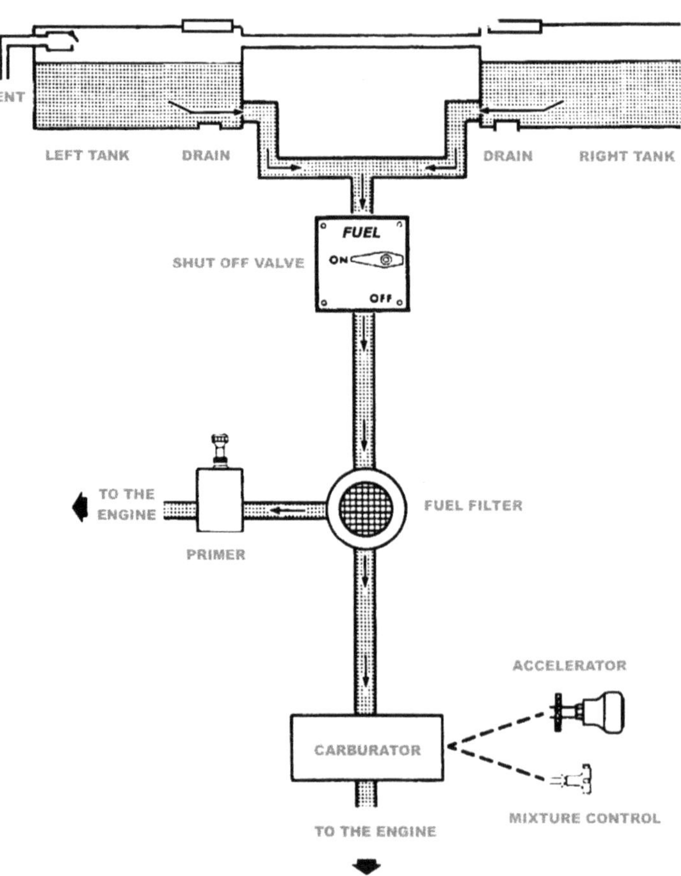

By observing the following image, we can see a real tank within its cavity inside the aircraft's wing. At its end, it features a manually operated fuel filler cap. Considering the possibility of replacing traditional tanks with long-range tanks, a modification of the cavity inside the wing would be required to accommodate a tank of larger dimensions than the traditional one.

Fuel venting and draining

Most fuel tanks in this class of aircraft are equipped with a venting system designed to eliminate gases that the fuel may emit, with the purpose of balancing the internal tank pressure with the external pressure. In most Cessna models, venting is represented by a tube located in the left-wing tank, just behind the strut.

The fuel system is equipped with a drain valve in each tank, allowing the pilot to extract fuel and assess its contamination level by dirt, water, or other pollutants. It is a drain valve with an opening for inserting a needle, which releases fuel into a transparent container to inspect its purity.

In addition to the drainage valve of each tank, there is a drainage control located in the engine in order to drain the fuel that

has already came out of the tank and is contained in the fuel circuit. This control can be seen and operated from the engine inspection cover.

Primer

The injector is a manual pump located in the left lower section of the instrument panel that connects the fuel line with all engine cylinders. When operating this pump, fuel is injected directly into the cylinders through the carburetor. This fuel injection is a normal requirement in a cold start, usually on the first flight of the day, in which the remaining fuel in the carburetor is not enough to supply the normal ignition cycle.

Fuel Indicators

This aircraft is equipped with two electric fuel indicators, one for each tank. Their operating principle is based on the measurement of the amount of fuel by means of floating devices that exert more or less pressure depending on the amount of liquid inside the tank. Depending on the aircraft position, the indication may vary due to the position of the float, which makes the actual indication of the fuel an approximate value, but not an accurate one.

Although the measurement system is mechanical, the information system is electrical. The first system will depend on the second one in flight or on its battery when the aircraft is parked. The indication of the amount of fuel can be represented in the number of gallons in each tank or as a percentage of total filling of the tanks. Let's look at some examples:

Other light aircraft use a pressure-feed system similar to the gravity system, but with the fuel supplied by a pressure pump. Fuel is drawn from the tanks by a mechanical or electric fuel pump through a tank selector and filter before being delivered to the carburetor.

Fuel injection to the engine is achieved using a **primer pump**, which draws fuel from the filter housing and delivers it to the intake manifold. The fuel system is monitored for content and pressure, and fuel drains allow for the removal of any water prior to flight.

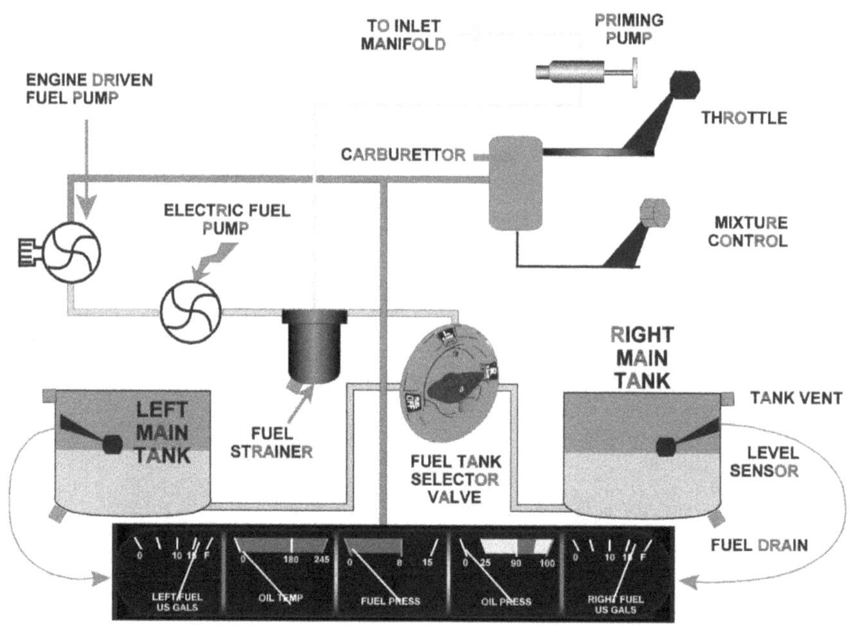

Multi-engine aircraft have more complex fuel systems to accommodate the additional requirements of altitude and engine configuration. Fuel tanks are invariably integral and located in the wings. Most modern aircraft may also have a "central tank," which is housed in the torque box of the central section between the wings.

The normal sequence of fuel use after takeoff would be to first use fuel from the central tank, followed by fuel from the wing tanks. This sequence helps to alleviate wing bending stress. When the booster pumps can no longer pump fuel from the central tank, the remaining fuel can be transferred to Tank No. 1 using the central tank scavenging system.

Fuel measurement

There are two methods for measuring the amount of fuel:

Volume measurement using a float to vary resistance, typically found in light aircraft. This method is subject to errors caused by aircraft maneuvers and cannot compensate for density variations.

Weight or mass measurement using capacitance, essential in modern passenger aircraft. This method is not affected by maneuvering errors and can compensate for density variations.

The capacitance method works by supplying AC current to the two plates of a capacitor. The current flowing through the circuit now depends on four factors: the applied voltage level, the supply frequency, the size of the plates, and the dielectric constant of the material separating the plates. In our circuit, three of these factors are fixed, and the fourth, the dielectric constant, is variable because the dielectric consists of fuel and air. The higher the fuel level in the tank, the more fuel and less air there will be in the capacitor probe, and vice versa.

Therefore, the amount of current flowing in the circuit depends on the amount of fuel/air between the plates, and by measuring this current, we can obtain an accurate indication of the fuel mass in the tanks.

The system can be made sensitive to the specific gravity (density) of the fuel so that, although the volume of a given quantity of fuel may increase with rising temperature, the resulting decrease in specific gravity ensures that the indicated mass (weight) remains the same.

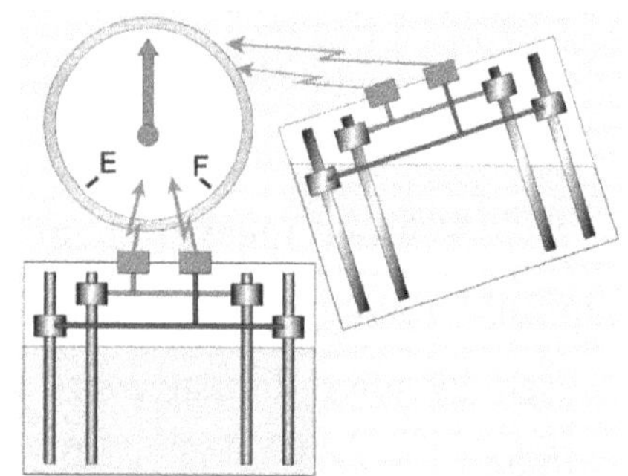

In the event of an electronic measurement system failure, we must be able to determine the fuel quantity manually. A dipstick can be used from the top of the tank, but this exposes the user to the inherent dangers of walking on high and slippery surfaces.

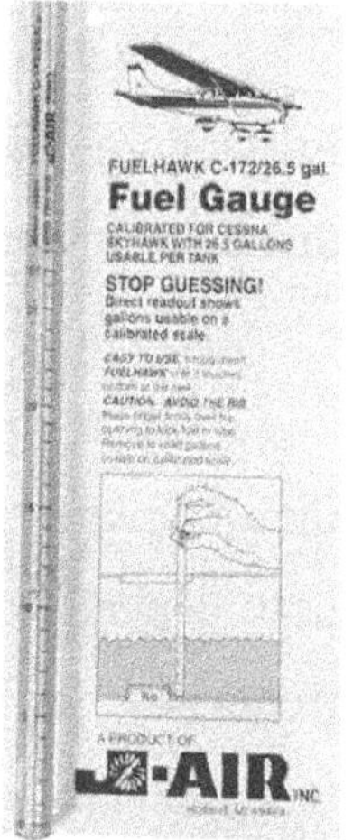

Fuel indicator

The instrumentation of the fuel system in a light aircraft will consist of fuel quantity and pressure gauges, but in large aircraft, it is necessary to provide information not only on fuel quantity and pressure but also on fuel used and valve positions, such as crossfeed valves. Other indications include the on/off status of the pumps and fuel temperature. These indicators are typically presented in the form of diagrams and lights electronically displayed.

The following figures show a typical display of the Airbus Centralized Electronic Aircraft Monitoring (ECAM) system and Boeing's Engine Indicating and Crew Alerting System (EICAS), both reporting everything necessary about the fuel system.

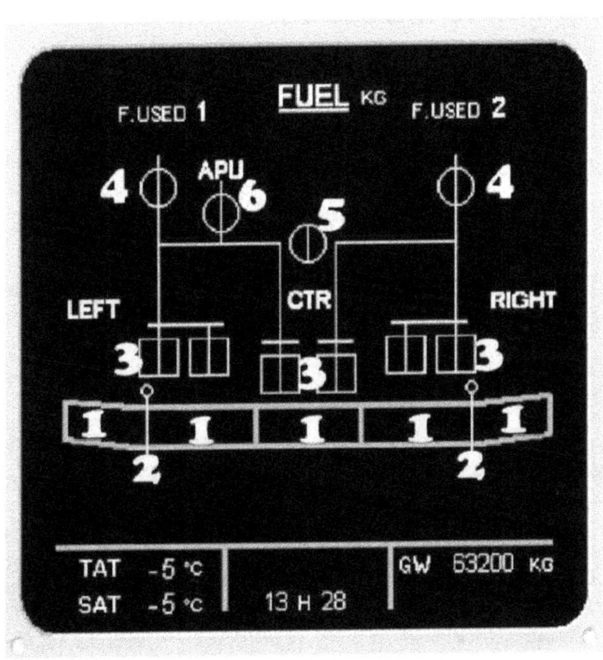

At **point 1**, the five fuel tanks are represented. At **point 2**, the two transfer valves. At **point 3**, the two fuel pumps in each tank. At **point 4**, the two low-pressure valves, one for each engine. At **point 5**, the crossfeed (XFEED) valve. And at **point 6**, the valve supplying fuel to the APU (Auxiliary Power Unit).

Fuel indications in a Boeing B737 are shown on the **Upper Display Unit (DU)**, located on the main panel, with different view options depending on the model and operator's preferences.

The information is typically displayed in the lower right corner of the DU (the location may vary based on the model) and can present various view options and measurement units:

Fuel flow pressure indication

The fuel flow pressure indication shows the same variables as the fuel quantity indication. It also provides a visual low-pressure alert on the indicator for each tank.

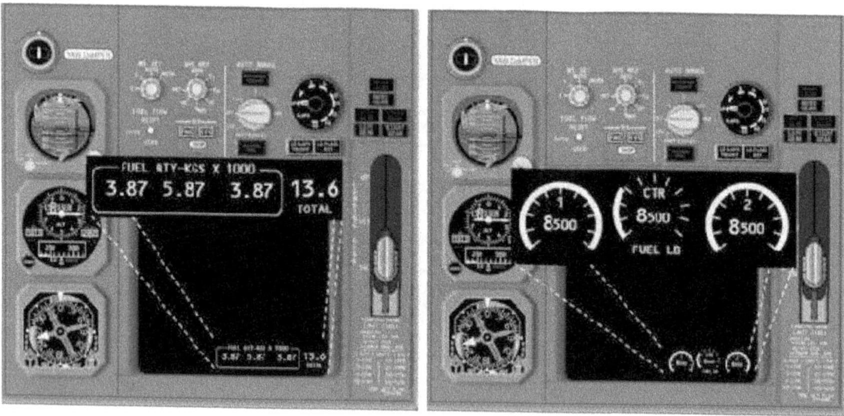

In the event that the system detects an imbalance of **1000 LBS or more** in the fuel quantities between the tanks, a visual alert will be triggered, similar to the previous low-pressure alert, but with the word **IMBAL** (imbalance) displayed over the information of the affected tank.

Chapter 6

Flight instruments

Biblioteca
Aeronáutica
aviación en simples pasos

Introduction

Before developing the operation of the aircraft's instruments, it is necessary to know the fundamental physical basis of the origin of the signals and the measurement methods. To do this, the principle of pitot tubes and static intakes is elaborated below.

Development must begin with a foundation of the fundamental principle, pressure. Pressure is a comparison between two forces. Absolute pressure exists when comparing a force with a total vacuum, or no absolute pressure. It is necessary to define absolute pressure, because the air in the atmosphere always exerts pressure, above all. Even when it seems that no pressure is being applied, such as when a balloon deflates, there is still atmospheric pressure inside and outside the balloon. To measure that atmospheric pressure, it is necessary to compare it with a total absence of pressure, such as that produced in a vacuum. Many aircraft instruments make use of absolute pressure values, such as the altimeter, the ascent speed indicator and the multiple pressure gauge.

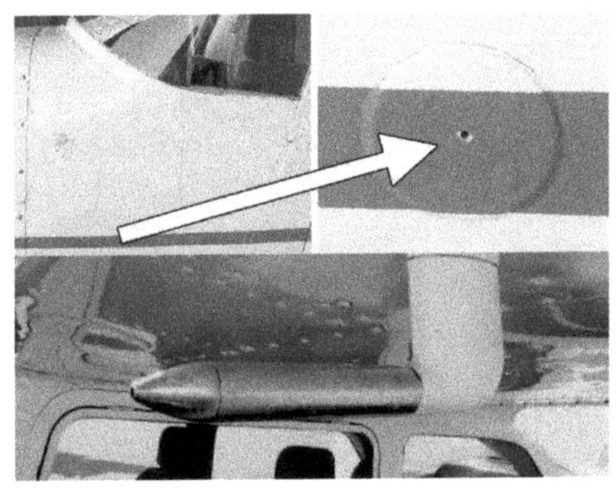

The most common type of pressure measurement is the gauge pressure. This expresses the difference between the pressure to be measured and atmospheric pressure. The gauge pressure inside the deflated balloon mentioned above is, therefore, 0 pounds per square inch (psi). The pressure of the pressure gauge is easily measured and obtained by ignoring the fact that the atmosphere always exerts its pressure, above all.

The pitot tube is a device that is used to establish the flow rate through the measurement of stagnation pressure or total pressure. The pressure is measured in a direction parallel to that of the flow and occluded at its other end that is equal to the sum of the static pressure and the dynamic pressure. Static pressure is the pressure of a fluid measured at one point. The total pressure is measured at the clogged end. Therefore, the value of the dynamic pressure that depends on the flow rate and its density is calculated by the difference between the measurements, in this case with the displacement of the diaphragm.

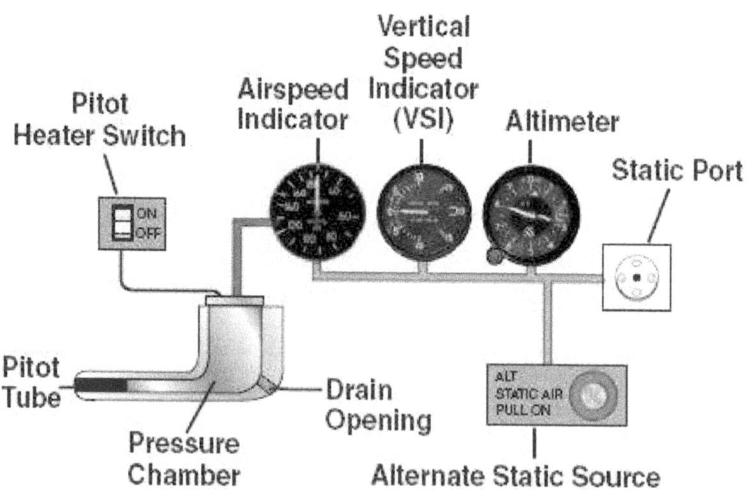

This device is used for flow measurement and consists of two tubes that detect pressure at two different points of the pipe.

They can be mounted separately or grouped within a housing, forming a single device. One of the tubes measures the impact pressure at one point in the vein, the other measures only the static pressure, usually through a hole in the conduction wall. A pitot tube measures two pressures simultaneously, impact pressure (pt) and static pressure (ps).

The Bernoulli Principle is the one that allows to establishing the pressure ratio and with it, be able to obtain a fundamental value for flight: aerodynamic speed.

Like pitot tubes, the static sockets are duplicated, and even tripled, in different places on the fuselage; to ensure a correct reading and maintain the criterion of redundancy and safety of the on-board systems.

Based on the above theory, it can be concluded that the three basic flight instruments are the speedometer, the variometer and the altimeter. The graph below shows its installation in the flight deck of a light aircraft typically used for instruction and training.

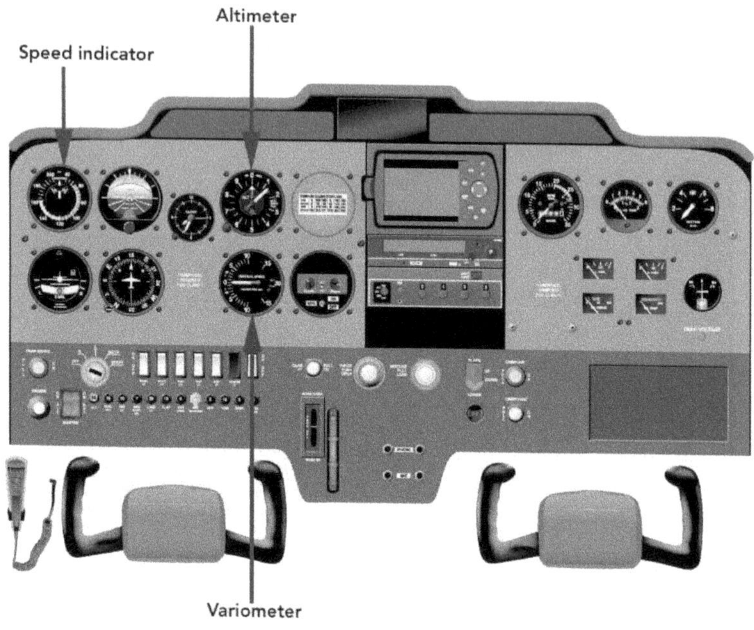

Partial, or total, obstructions in pitot tubes and static intakes entail erroneous readings on the instruments, a fact that drastically damages the safety of the flight. When a pitot tube is blocked and the static intake is free, at least one of the following failures will occur:

Probably the speedometer will be set to zero, due to the lack of dynamic pressure input.

The behavior of the speedometer will resemble an altimeter, when the drainage of the incoming pressure is clogged. The reading that the pilot will have will be: increase in the speed in ascent and fall of the speed in descent. In all cases, the readings are wrong.

A pitot block should not affect the reading of the variometer, or the altimeter.

When the blockage is found in the static sockets, it is very likely that errors will occur in the reading of the speedometer, variometer and altimeter. The following are the most likely occurrence failures:

Altimeter lock. The reading it will show will be constant and in line with the last reading before blocking; this occurs due to the lack of changes in static pressure.

The variometer will also be locked in a fixed indication, as will the altimeter due to the lack of static pressure.

The speedometer will tend to mark a lower aerodynamic speed than the real one.

If the blockage occurs in the pitot and the static intake at the same time, the three instruments (speedometer, variometer and altimeter) will mark zero.

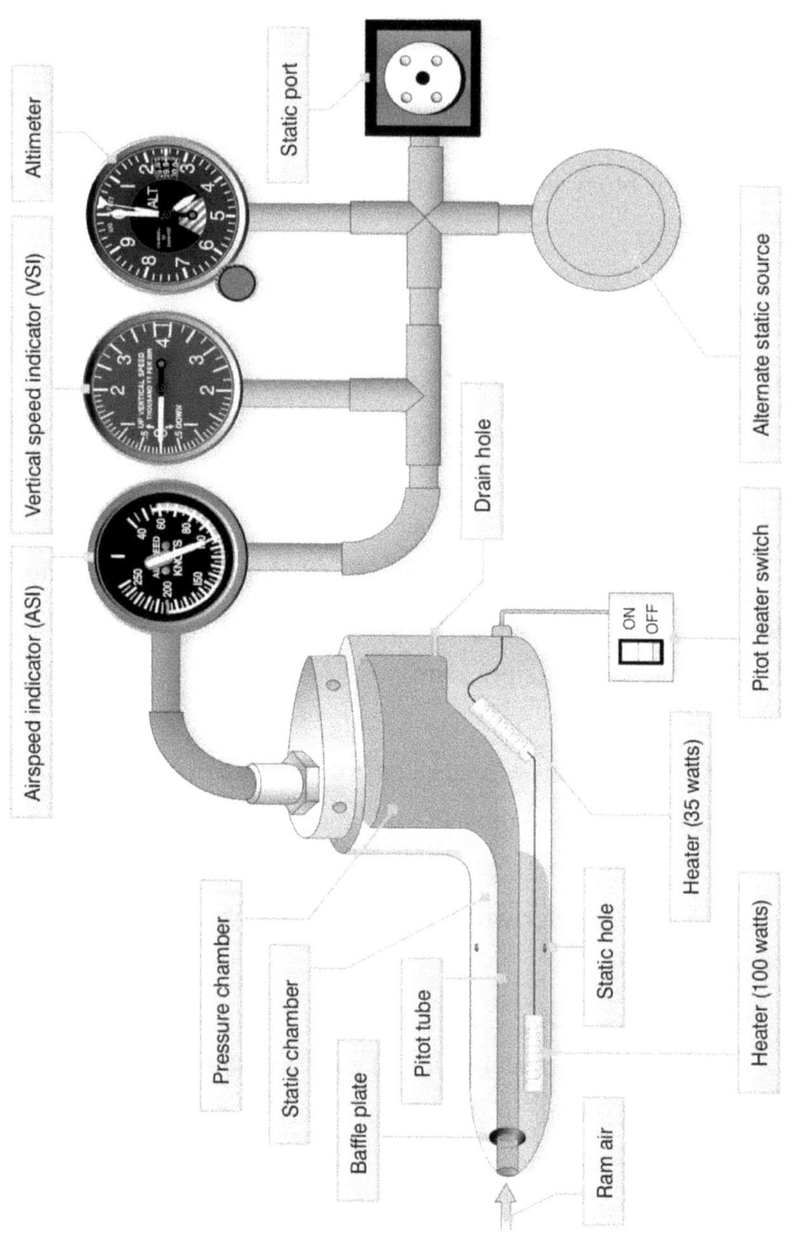

Excerpt from the FAA (federal aviation administration) flight instrument document

In this graph (excerpt from FAA federal aviation administration) you can see the summary scheme of the entry and measurement of pressure in a light aircraft. At the same time, an electrical heating system (electrical resistance) is observed that prevents the accumulation of ice in the pilot when the aircraft is in flight.

Altimeter

An analog altimeter, like the one shown in the previous figure works with the same principle as a clock, with two hands, it works with the same principle as a clock, with two hands. It has a dial marked with numbers from 0 to 9, arranged clockwise, with intermediate divisions. The instrument is made up of a closed cylindrical box, inside which is arranged an aneroid capsule, made of very thin metal (usually copper).

The aneroid capsule is pre-filled with a standard atmospheric pressure (1013.2 Hp or mmHg). The altimeter has a port through which atmospheric pressure enters (from the static intake), therefore, there will be a difference in pressures between the reading of the static intake and that present in the aneroid capsule.

The altimeters have two needles. The longest needle indicates thousands of feet, while the second one indicates hundreds. In this type of altimeter, a full turn of the larger needle indicates that 10,000 feet were won or lost (depending on the direction of rotation). In altimeters that have three needles, the third and shorter indicates tens of a thousand.

According to the previous paragraphs, the altitude reading is a difference in pressures. Therefore, it is necessary that the altimeter be calibrated according to the place of operation of the aircraft and other operational peculiarities that will be described. To this end, all altimeters have a manual control device that allows the internal aneroid capsule to be dilated or contracted, with the aim of decreasing or increasing the value of the internal reference pressure.

The variation in the volume of the capsule responds to the fundamental principle of Boyle-Marriot that expresses "... the value of the pressure is inversely proportional to the volume...". This calibration is known as an "altimeter setting". To verify the correction value, all altimeters have a graduated window, which allows you to see the adjustment reference; this device is known as the adjustment window or “Kollsman".

The image below shows the cutting of a mechanical analog pressure altimeter; an instrument that equips the vast majority of general aviation aircraft. In the cut, you can see the detail of the aneroid capsule and the mechanical connection with the set of gears and connecting rods that allow the movement and indication to be transmitted to the needles on the quadrant of the instrument.

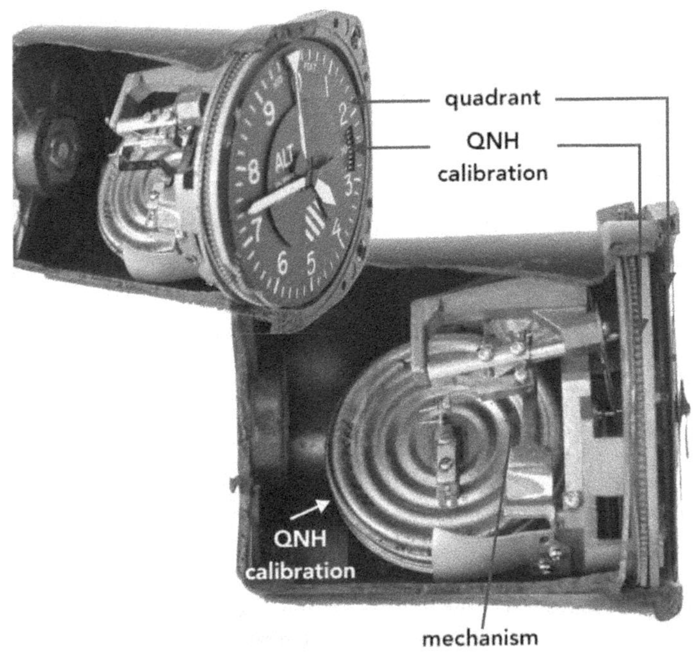

As can be seen in the previous image, the aneroid capsule is located in a closed container (cut of the shell seen in the image) where it receives external pressure, through a flexible duct with connection to the static intake. The actual pressure from the outside will be responsible for the expansion or contraction of the capsule. The set of gears and associated connecting rods are those that transmit the movement and transform it into a calibrated angular movement; which, in turn, is then transformed into altitude reading for the crew.

For the calibration of the altimeter, it is necessary to consider different pressure values. The values correspond to the place of operation, reference at the level of the evil, and specific pressure of a point. These pressure reference values are expressed as follows:

QNH: it is the value of the pressure referred to sea level. In this case, with the aircraft on the ground, the altimeter will indicate the altitude at which the aerodrome is located.

QNE: it is the representation of the pressure referred to the flight level, that is, it is the adjustment that indicates the distance from the ground to the reference pressure of the aneroid capsule.

QFE: it is the specific pressure at a point in the earth's crust, in the case of the aircraft, it will be the actual pressure that exists at the aerodrome at the time of the start of the operation.

It is also important to mention other types of altimeters specially designed for ultralight, experimental, gyroplane aircraft, among others. To do this, the Tasken 5000 altimeter (or similar) can be mentioned. This type of digital altimeter, unlike mechanical altimeters is not affected by the high vibration of two-stroke engines that are frequently used in ultralight aircraft. Two-stroke or four-stroke motors (non-aeronautical or modified) introduce a vibration level that adversely alters the operation of the internal mechanical assembly of traditional analog instruments.

The solid-state altimeter can withstand severe shocks and vibrations, while maintaining the accuracy of your indication. It has a 4.5-digit full liquid crystal (LCD) screen with large characters 1/2" high. Because the LCD screen uses a

direct drive, it is easily readable from most viewing angles and does not disappear when viewed from an angle or is not washed in full sun.

The Tasken 5000 model includes a backlight to watch at night or dusk. The altitude range extends from below sea level to well above the need for additional oxygen. The limits range from -1000 to 19990 feet (-305 to 6093 meters). The increments are in steps of 10 feet or 1 m. The instrument is powered by DC in the range of 730 V and is protected from accidental polarity reversal. A 9V battery is a common power supply and a battery holder for this is provided on the back, external to the housing. An alkaline battery will provide more than 40 hours of operation, without the illuminated backlight. The backlight does not turn on in the ON position of the power switch to preserve battery life.

Radio altimeter

A radio altimeter is a device that measures the actual vertical distance of the aircraft from the terrain. It works in a similar way to radar, emits a signal pulse, which bounces against the surface of the ground, returns to the receiver and the system computes the distance according to the time elapsed between the emission and the reception of the signal.

Radio altimeter is mainly used during an instrument approach and on low-level or night flights below 3000 to 2500 feet (depending on the characteristics of the equipment). This system provides the primary altitude information for the landing decision height. It incorporates an adjustable altitude error that creates a visual or audio warning for the pilot when the plane reaches that altitude. Usually, the pilot will abort a landing if the decision height is reached and the runway is not visible.

Using a transceiver and a directional antenna, a radio altimeter emits a carrier wave at 4.3 gHz from the aircraft directly to the ground. The wave is modulated in frequency at 50 mHz and travels at a known speed. It hits the orography of the surface and bounces toward the plane where a second antenna receives the return signal. The transceiver processes the signal by measuring the elapsed time and the frequency modulation that occurred. The screen indicates the height above the ground, also known as above ground level (AGL).

A radar altimeter is more accurate and sensitive than an air pressure altimeter to obtain AGL information at low altitudes. The transceiver is usually far from the indicator. Multifunctional cabin screens usually integrate the decision height awareness of the radar altimeter as a digital number that is displayed on the screen with an error, light or color change used to indicate when that altitude is reached.

Similarly, the radio altimeter works the same as a DME, but vertically. It is neither more nor less than a radar that emits at an angle of 90° with respect to the aircraft where it is installed. That is why it is a device that is also associated with proximity alert systems with the terrain of the TAWS type or the most evolved ones such as the Ground Proximity Warning System - GPWS.

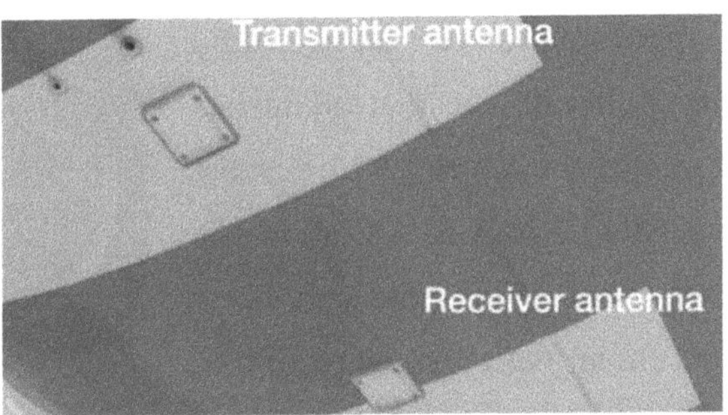

As can be seen in the image above, the system has two antennas, the one that emits and the one it receives, unlike the radar that concentrates everything in a single device.

In aircraft of large size or equipped with integrated avionics systems (it is worth the previous example of the Boeing 737-700), radio altimeter information is presented on the Primary Flight Display - PFD, as shown in this image. The screenshot of a PFD can be seen

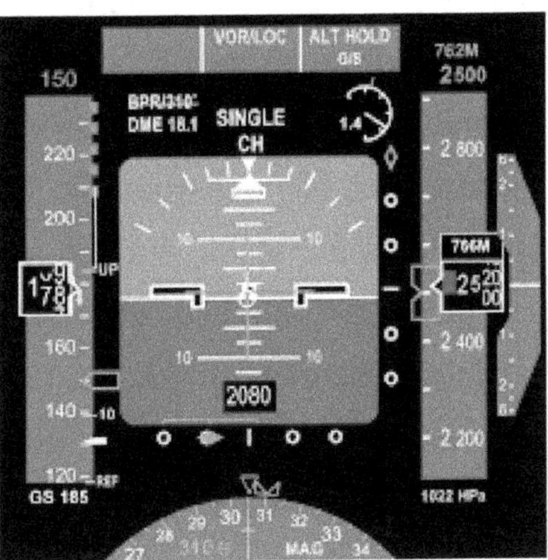

in the previous image. On the right side, two altitude readings are identified, in the upper right margin (2500) the radiometer reading is shown; while in the lateral band (2520) there is the reading of the altimetric baro altitude.

Airspeed indicator

The speedometer or aerodynamic speed indicator is the device that quantifies the relative speed of the aircraft with respect to the air mass where it moves. Aerodynamic speed is an expression of relationships, not a speed of displacement with respect to a point on the ground (ground speed).

The speedometer is a device that measures the pressure differences and transforms them into units of speed (knots, miles per hour, etc.). The differential value between the impact pressure or total pressure and the static pressure value is the value that will be converted into aerodynamic speed. As a general concept for understanding operation, it is said that the greater the pressure difference, the greater the aerodynamic speed. Like the altimeter, the speedometer has a barometric capsule inside it that maintains the impact pressure inside through a connection port with the pitot tube. The pressure difference between the inside and outside of the aneroid capsule generates shrinkage or expansion of the material. This movement is captured by the internal clockwork system that translates it into the movement of the hand on the dial of the instrument. Just as the example of the altimeter was made, below is an image of a fully disassembled speedometer in its sealed container housing. In this case, it is observed that the pressure census capsule is located on the back of the instrument. At the back of the capsule there are two ports through which the pressure of the impact air mass and the static pressure enter.

Through that pressure, the instrument generates the expansion and contraction of the capsule, which transmits the movement towards the gears and set of internal connecting rods; which will then be responsible for generating the angular movement of the only needle that will move in the graduated quadrant (in this case the reading is done in miles per hour, along with a dial that allows you to see the conversion into knots).

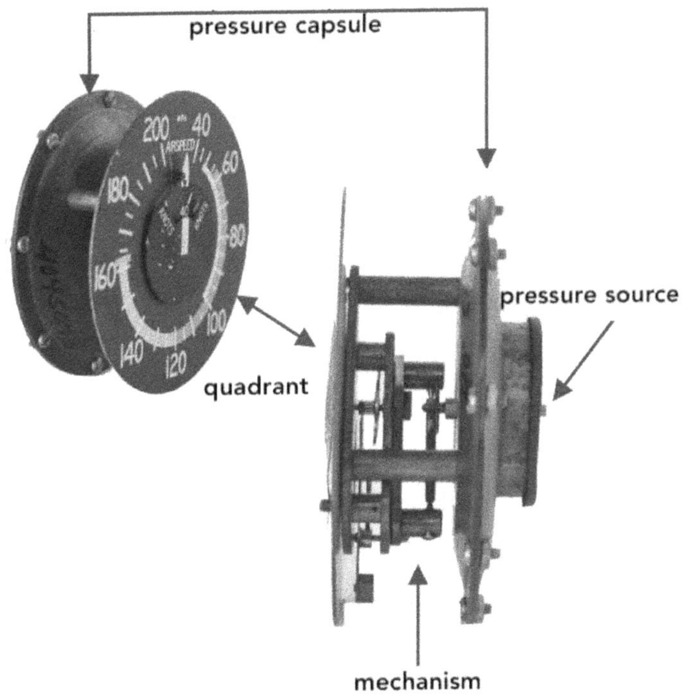

Due to the direct reading due to the pressure variation, the aerodynamic speed shown by the instrument is called: indicated speed (IAS or KIAS - Knots Indicated Airspeed). IAS is the speed that most manufacturers consider in the design and publication of the performances and limitations of an aircraft, among the most common can be mentioned:

- Speeds never to exceed
- Flaps extension speed
- Stall speed
- Minimal control speed
- Limiting maneuvering speeds

There are also other speeds that are necessary to know for the safe operation of the aircraft.

Calibrated Airspeed (CAS): this is the value of the IAS corrected for possible errors in the instrument. Speed calibration is obtained through calculations and tables. Operation and flight manuals usually include indicative tables and graphs for the conversion and calculation of calibrated speed.

Equivalent Speed (EAS - Equivalent Airspeed): it is the expression of the calibrated speed with the correction of the potential error due to the effect of the adiabatic compressibility of the air mass (high speed flight) and the effect of altitude.

True Airspeed (TAS): TAS is a magnitude of aerodynamic speed (IAS) that cannot be measured directly by the instrument. At low speed, true velocity is an expression that is the product of the equivalent velocity (CAS) by the root of the pressure density quotient. When the speed exceeds relative 100 kt, the TAS must be calculated based on the Mach number; in this case, the TAS is the product of the Mach velocity at the root of the static air temperature ratio and the relative ratio at average sea level.

Variometer

It is the flight instrument that provides information related to two variables of the aircraft, closely related to each other: the movement of ascent or descent and the regime or rate with which it does so, better known as vertical speed.

The operating principle of the variometer is similar to that of the altimeter. The marking on the dial is generated by the contraction and expansion movement of an aneroid capsule in contact with the external pressure of the air. The difference with the altimeter is that the variometer does not measure the absolute pressure, but records the pressure changes coming from the static intake of the fuselage; it does not need dynamic pressure reading. The set of aneroid capsule and watch system is located inside a closed and insulated container, in the same way as the speedometer and the altimeter.

The variometer has a single needle that marks on a dial with a scale that begins at zero (located to the left of the quadrant of the instrument). The reading is simple, all the marks that are above zero indicate ascent, while those located below show a descent regime. In light aircraft, variometers with scales and marks representing 100 feet per minute (ppm) are used.

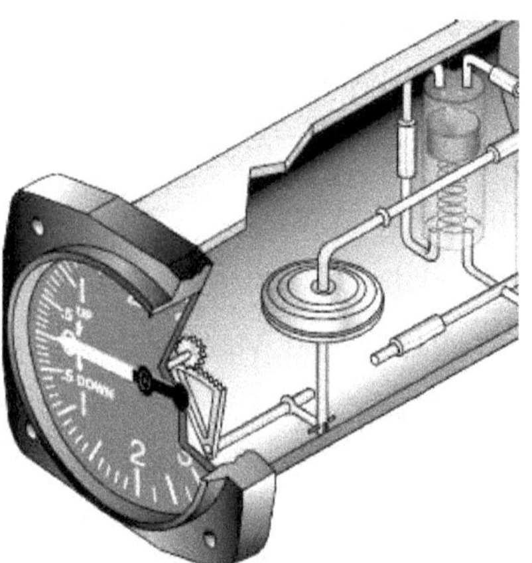

In the event that there is a failure in the static pressure takeover system, the variometer will be blocked at the last reading, or it may give erroneous readings in case of partial obstructions of the area or the shot.

In extreme cases, where the crew is reliably aware of the failure that occurs, breaking the instrument's glass will provide the device with the actual static pressure value. When it has a differential pressure again, the aneroid capsule will return with its expansion and expansion mechanics; a fact that will allow the instrument to give real values again.

Attitude indicator

The artificial horizon (or attitude indicator), is one of the essential flight instruments. This provides the pilot with pitching and balancing information, which is especially important when flying without external visual references. The attitude indicator works with a gyroscope that rotates in the horizontal plane. Therefore, it imitates the real horizon, through its rigidity in space. As the aircraft swings and rotates in relation to the real horizon, the gyroscope gimbals allow the aircraft and the instrument housing to swing and rotate around the gyroscope rotor that remains parallel to the ground. A horizontal representation of the miniature aircraft is fixed to the instrument housing.

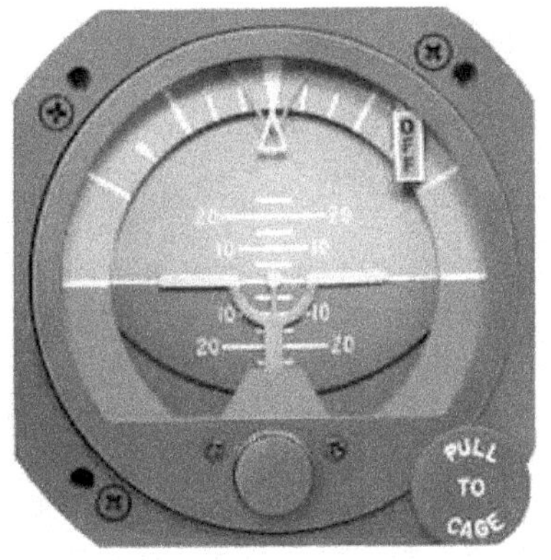

A painted hemisphere that simulates the horizon, the sky and the ground, is attached to the gyroscopic gimbals. The sky and the ground meet in what is called the horizon bar. The relationship between the horizon bar and the miniature plane is the same as that of the plane and the real horizon. The graduated scales refer to the degrees of pitching and balancing. Often, an adjustment knob allows pilots of different heights to place the horizon bar at an appropriate level.

In a gyroscopic vacuum-driven attitude system, the air is sucked through a filter and then through the attitude indicator, in a way that rotates the gyroscope rotor inside it. A mounting mechanism has been incorporated into the instrument to help maintain the rotation of the gyroscopic rotor in the intended plane. The precession caused by the friction of the bearing makes it necessary. After the air is applied to the drive around the rotor, it flows from the instrument to the vacuum pump, through four ports. All these ports expel the same amount of air, when the gyroscope rotates on the plane. When the gyroscope rotates outside the plane, the air tends to come out from one side more than the other. The fins close to avoid this, which causes more air to come out of the opposite side. The force of this unequal air ventilation reassembles the gyroscopic rotor.

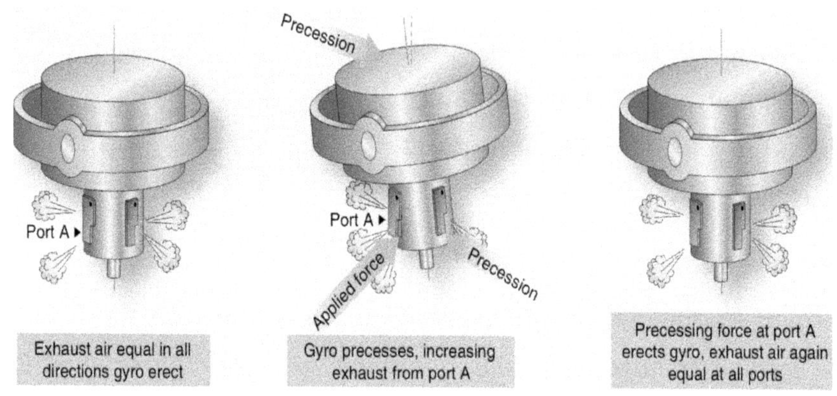

In the previous figure, the internal system of the artificial horizon is represented, where the gyroscope principles are combined with the pressure action. Representation published in the document of the Federal Aviation Administration FAA-H-8083-31 "Aviation Maintenance Technical Handbook-Airframe".

The first vacuum-driven attitude indicators were limited in terms of the distance at which the aircraft could tilt or roll, before the gyroscope gimbals stopped, causing an abrupt precession and a fall of the gyroscope.

A flag indicates that the gyroscope must be caged before use. There are more modern gyroscopic instruments so that they do not fall, regardless of the angular movement of the plane on its axes.

In addition to the potential for pollution introduced by the air drive system, there are other deficiencies in the performance of vacuum-driven attitude indicators. Some are induced by the erection mechanism. The pendulum blades that move to direct the air flow outside the gyroscope respond not only to the forces caused by a deviation from the planned plane of rotation, but the centrifugal force experienced during the turns also means that the blades allow the asymmetric transport of the vacuum air of the gyroscope.

The result is an inaccurate visualization of the attitude of the plane, especially in drifts and sharp curves. In addition, sudden acceleration and deceleration impose forces on the gyroscopic rotor. Suspended in his gimbals, he acts in a similar way to an accelerometer, resulting in a false indication of nose up or nose down. Pilots must learn to recognize these errors and adjust them accordingly.

Considering the same criterion as that expressed in the development of the speedometer compared to light or experimental aircraft, there are also solid-state artificial horizon devices, although they do not have the precision of traditional equipment; they are effective for this type of aircraft.

Turn and bank indicator

The turn indicator, commonly known as a "stick-ball", is the instrument used to coordinate the turns of the aircraft. The turn and slide indicator are, in fact, two separate devices, integrated into the same instrument housing: a turn indicator and a sliding indicator. The rotation indicator is operated by a gyroscope, which can be driven by a vacuum pump, air pressure or electricity.

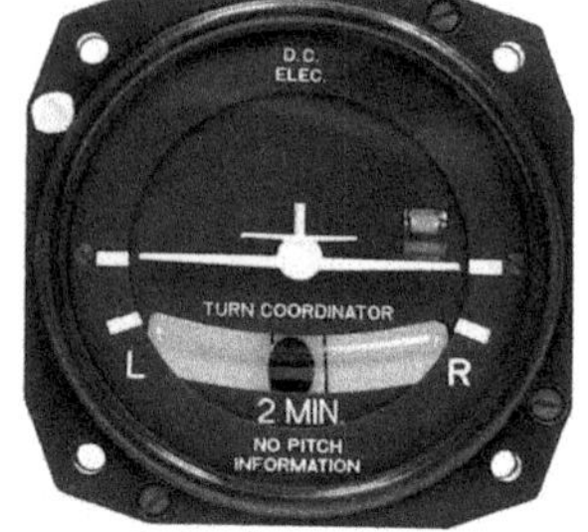

The ball is a completely independent device. It is a round agate, or steel ball, in a glass tube filled with non-viscous moisturizing liquid. It moves in response to gravity, and the centrifugal force experienced in a turn. The movement of the ball in the liquid works with the same principle as the air bubble, in a level tool used in the construction industry.

The turn indicators reflect the speed at which the plane rotates. Three degrees of rotation per second, make an airplane rotate 360 degrees in 2 minutes. This is considered a standard turn. This speed can be indicated with marks to the right and left of the pointer or reference aircraft represented on the instrument. Sometimes, there are no marks present and the width of the pointer is used as a calibration device. In this case, the deviation of the width of a pointer from the vertical is equal to the standard rotation speed of 2 minutes of 3 ° per second. Faster planes tend to spin more slowly and have graduations or labels that indicate 4-minute turns.

In other words, the width or alignment of a pointer with a tick mark on this instrument indicates that the plane is spinning 1o1⁄2 per second and completes a 360 ° turn in 4 minutes. It is common to label the face of the instrument with words indicating whether it is a 2- or 4-minute turn indicator.

The rotation pointer indicates the speed at which an airplane rotates on its vertical axis. This is achieved by virtue of the precession of a gyroscope to tilt a pointer. The gyroscope rotates in a vertical plane aligned with the longitudinal axis of the aircraft. When the plane rotates on its vertical axis during a rotation, the force experienced by the rotating gyro compass is exerted on the vertical axis. Due to the precession, the reaction of the gyroscope rotor is 90 ° more around the gyroscope in the direction of rotation. This means that the reaction to the force around the vertical axis is the movement around the longitudinal axis of the aircraft.

The phenomenon described above causes the top of the rotor to tilt to the left or right. The pointer is joined by a link that causes the pointer to deviate in the opposite direction, which matches the direction of rotation. Then, the rotation of the plane around the vertical axis is indicated around the longitudinal axis on the meter. This is intuitive for the pilot when it comes to the instrument, since the pointer indicates in the same direction as the turn.

The part of the slide indicator (ball) of the instrument is an inclinometer. The ball responds only to gravity during coordinated flight in a straight and level line. Therefore, rest on the lowest part of the curved glass between the reference cables. When a turn is started and the plane is inclined, both the gravity and the centrifugal force of the turn act on the ball. If the turn is coordinated, the ball remains in place. If there is a sliding rotation, the centrifugal force exceeds the force of gravity on the ball and moves in the direction of the outside of the rotation. During a sliding turn, there is more inclination than necessary and gravity is greater than the centrifugal force that acts on the ball. The ball moves in the curved glass into the turn.

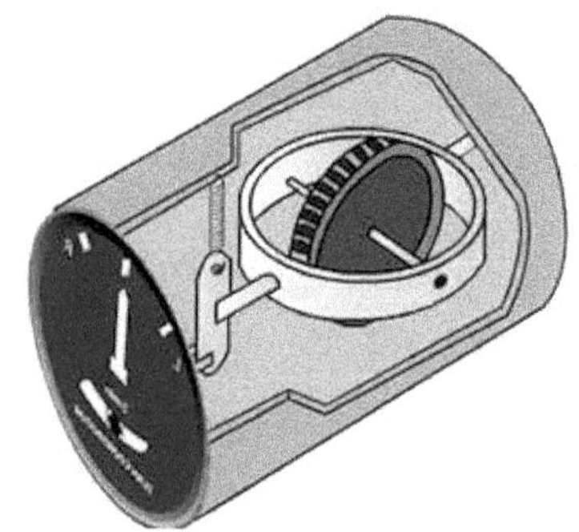

As mentioned above, the energy for the gyroscope turn and slip indicator is often electric if the attitude and direction indicators work with vacuum. This allows limited battery-free operation if the vacuum system and the electric generator fail. The directional and attitude information of the turn and slide indicator, combined with the information of the static pitot instruments, allow a continuous and safe emergency operation of the aircraft.

VOR - VHF Omnidirectional Range

Its Spanish translation is omnidirectional radio headlight of very high frequency. It is a widely used system since the end of World War II, which is still the basis of radio navigation today. The VOR combines a ground station with a dialing receiver on the aircraft. The Earth station emits signals on VHF frequency (usually band between 108.00 and 117.95 mHz), the signals of the station corresponds to one emission beam for each of the points of the wind rose. That is, the VOR emits a signal in each of the 360 degrees that make up the rose (at intervals of 10 in 10 generally). Depending on the type of frequency used, a VOR station has a range of around 320 km and an altitude of 37,500 feet. The VOR works like a marine beacon, only instead of emitting a light signal that can be seen from a distance by ships; it emits radio signals that are picked up by an aircraft's antenna.

VOR stations or stations are located in airports and aerodromes, as well as at key points on the navigation routes. These points are also known as “fixed". The radio frequency emitted by a VOR contains or is modulated by three signals. One is the identification of the station in Morse code, which allows the pilot to identify it. The other two signal sources come from 30 Hz whose phases vary from each other. They are called reference signals and variable signal respectively. The reference always keeps each phase constant, while the variable changes its phase according to the direction in which it is emitted. The direction is measured by its azimuth, that is, it is divided 360 degrees around the VOR antenna counting clockwise from the Earth's magnetic north, is a point at which the reference signal and the variable have identical phases. In this way, a VOR antenna can be displayed as the point from which 360 lines of direction depart, which are called radials.

The instrument located in the cockpit interprets the signal, according to the frequency selected by the pilot. When the chosen radial is located in the direction of advance of the aircraft, the "TO" indication will be activated, once the aircraft has left the selected station behind, the "FROM" indication will be activated on the dial (or information screen). If you do not have the radio intercepted, it does not necessarily indicate whether the aircraft is heading to or from the station.

The device that indicates whether the signal is correct or unreliable is the so-called "OFF" flag. It retracts from the view of the instrument when the signal strength is sufficient to provide reliable indications on the instrument. Alternatively, an insufficient signal strength is indicated by a blank space or a flag on the instrument. To fly directly to the station, the selector knob - Omni Bearing Selector (OBS) - must be rotated until the CDI is centered with the indication "to". Then the pilot flies that direction. To know the radial of the VOR that crosses the aircraft, it is enough to center the CDI with the indication "from". If a specific radial is selected on the instrument, the CDI will be on the right or left either with the indication "to" or "from". The direction of the aircraft does not affect this selection.

ADF - Automatic Direction Finder

It is one of the first radio aid systems for navigation, which is still in use today. The ADF installed on board the aircraft receives the signal from a terrestrial antenna (NDB - Non Directional Beacon) that transmits at amplitude modulated frequencies in a range of 190 to 450 kHz. The ADF consists of two antennas, both for reception. The system is composed of a pair of antennas that process the information, to provide the reading on the cockpit instrument.

The non-directional antenna receives radio signals with almost the same intensity from all directions. The "cyclic" antenna receives radio signals with more power than only two directions (bidirectional). When the signals from both antennas are processed, it is possible to receive a radio signal in all but one direction, thus resolving the ambiguity.

The basic concept of radio compass is that of an indicator on the cabin instrument that points to the station and thus shows the position of the aircraft with the station. This ratio is known as relative marking regardless of the direction of the aircraft, the indicator needle will show the relative marking. The VOR indicator will be centered when the plane is on the selected radial, but regardless of the direction. The needle of the ADF will be in the center only when the station is right in front of the plane, in this way, the fundamental thing about this radio help is that it provides information about the direction in which the station is located.

The ADF is a navigation support team for systems that operate on VHF. Therefore, it is possible to use it when this type of visual range wave-based navigation is not possible. The radio beats when working on the LF and MF bands. The presentation of the instrument in the information is done in two ways:

Radio Bearing Indicator (RBI): this instrument always indicates zero (north course) on the dial, in a compass or wind rose format. This type of instrument has a fixed dial and dialing is the direct reading of the direction or position from which the NDB signal is received.

Rotary dial ADF: the operation is analogous to that of the RBI, only in this case the pilot has a device that allows him to rotate the dial or primer. Through this position selection, the pilot can align the dial with the actual course of the aircraft.

DME - Distance Measurement Equipment

It is a basic system that literally measures the distance of the aircraft, with respect to a ground station, which emits a radio signal. The frequencies used by DME systems range from 962 to 1213 mHz (UHF band); each equipment has the ability to handle 200 channels. Usually, the information provided by the DME system is associated with the VOR equipment, ADF, instrumental approach system, among others.

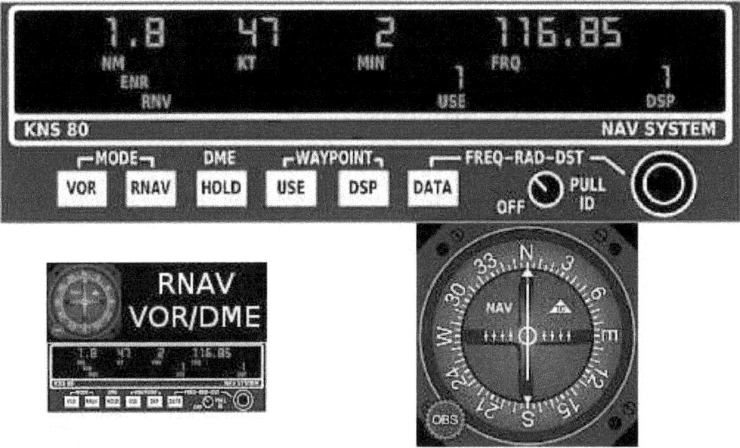

When used in conjunction with the VOR system, the DME allows the pilot to determine an exact geographical position of the aircraft, including the direction and distance to or from the station. The DME of the aircraft interrogates using a radio frequency signal, which are received by the DME antenna in the ground facilities. The DME of the aircraft measures the time elapsed between the interrogation signal sent by the aircraft and the receipt of the response from the ground station.

This time measurement is converted into the distance in nautical miles (NM) of the station. It should be noted that the distance measured by the DME is the distance is the inclined distance, directly from the aircraft to the station, which differs from the actual distance on the ground, which is generally less than the distance measured by the DME. That difference increases as the aircraft approaches the station. Some DME receivers provide a ground speed (GS - Ground Speed) in knots through the relative movement of the aircraft relative to the ground station. These ground speed values are accurate only when the aircraft is heading directly to or from the station.

RMI - Radio Magnetic Indicator

The RMI is the system that replaces the ADF in terms of functionality and improvements in operation and performance. This instrument combines information from a radio frequency and magnetic orientation (beginning of the bar or basic compass); providing the pilot with concrete information about the direction, course and radial in which he is flying.

The dial or primer is based on a directional gyroscopic device that rotates automatically with the aircraft's turns. Therefore, this instrument provides adequate and accurate information on the direction of the plane and the magnetic direction to the station.

The RMI differs from the ADF to a rotary primer, in that it is not necessary to update the course of the aircraft manually. When the needle is selected to work with the VOR receivers, the upper end of the needle indicates the direction towards the ground station and the tail indicates the radial in which the aircraft is located. Most RMI equipment allows you to choose which receiving antennas each needle works with. At the bottom of the instrument there are knobs or buttons to change the indication of the needles, be it ADF or VOR.

HSI - Horizontal Situation Indicator

The horizontal location indicator is a device that combines a gyroscopic device (magnetic compass) with the functions of a VOR. This instrument provides information related to the selected flight course.

The arrowhead indicating the course is selected at 090°; the tail of this needle indicates the reciprocal radial, 270°. The course deviation bar (CDI) operates with a VOR/locator receiver (VOR/ LOC) to indicate left or right deviations of the selected course. The desired course is selected by rotating the course selection knob.

The location of the aircraft figure and the CDI bar show the deviation of the aircraft from the course that was originally selected, as if the pilot were above the aircraft looking down.

The "TO/FROM" indicator is a triangular pointer (as in the always VOR instrument). When the indicator points to the head of the course arrow, it is shown that the selected course, if the CDI is centered, takes the aircraft to the tuned station.

When the indicator points to the tail of the arrow, it takes the aircraft in the opposite direction to the selected station. The glideslope pointer indicates the relationship of the aircraft to the glide path (during the instrumental approach operation or ILS). When the pointer is below the central position, the aircraft is above the glide path, and a higher vertical descent speed is required.

RBT - Radar Beacon Transponder

It is a "responder" device. Literally, it is a team that responds to the interrogation of the secondary terrestrial radar system (SSR - Secondary Sourvillance Radar) and TCAS systems of other transits, emitting a signal with information about the aircraft: flight identification (responder code), flight level, speed and condition of ascent or descent. The signal emitted by the on-board transponder is captured by the secondary radar antenna, and then represents that information on the radar screen of the aerial controller.

The air traffic controller uses a secondary surveillance radar (SSR) to verify the position of the aircraft and add the third dimension of altitude to its location. The SSD radar transmits encoded pulse sets or packages that are received by the transponder on board the aircraft. Mode 3 A impulses, as they are known, help confirm the location of the aircraft. When verbal communication is established with the air traffic controller, the pilot is instructed to select one of the 4096 codes on the transponder. These are digital codes.

The Earth station transmits a pulse of energy and the transponder transmits a response with the assigned code attached. This confirms the location of the aircraft by altering its target symbol on the radar screen. Since the screen can be full of many confirmed aircraft, the air traffic controller can also ask the pilot to identify himself. When you press the IDENT button on the transponder, it is transmitted in such a way that the symbol of the aircraft's target is highlighted on the screen to distinguish it.

To obtain altitude clarification, the transponder control must be placed in the ALT or Mode C position. The signal transmitted back to the air traffic controller, in response to the interrogation of the pulse, is modified with a code that places the pressure altitude of the aircraft next to the target symbol on the radar screen.

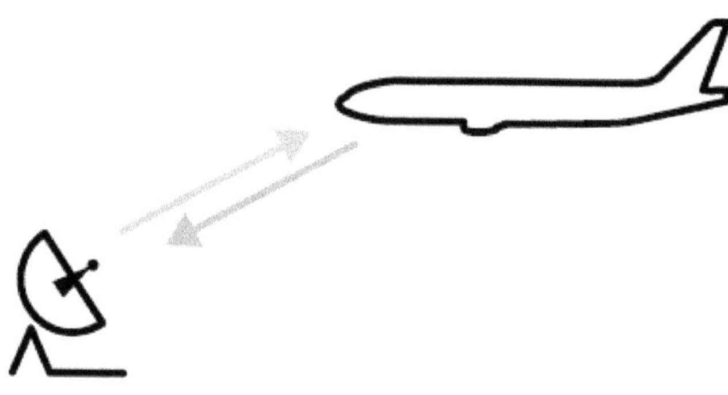

The transponder system of the aircraft described is known as the air traffic control radar beacon system (ATCRBS). To improve the safety conditions, the altitude response has been developed in Mode S. With Mode S, each aircraft is previously assigned a unique identity code, which is displayed along with its pressure altitude on the radar when the transponder responds to the SSR question. Since no other aircraft responds with this code, the possibility for two pilots to select the same response code on the transponder is eliminated. A modern computer with a flight data processor (FDP) assigns the beacon code and searches the flight plan data for useful information that will be displayed on the screen next to the target, in a block of data for each aircraft.

S mode is sometimes also known as mode selection. It is a data package that is also used in collision prevention systems on board. When used by an air traffic controller, S mode interrogates one aircraft at a time. The workload of the transponder is reduced, since it does not have to answer all interrogations in an airspace. In addition, location information is more accurate with S Mode. A single response in which the response phase of the transponder is used to calculate the position, called a single pulse, is enough to locate the aircraft.

TCAS - Traffic Collision Avoidance System

The in-flight collision prevention system (TCAS) is composed of equipment based on the operation of the on-board transponders. The TCAS processes the signals of the responders of the aircraft that are within the airspace surrounding the aircraft, and generates an indication as to the possibility of approach, distance and attitude of the other traffics. Currently there are two types of TCAS: TCAS I and TCAS II. The TCAS I system was developed to provide a defense to the general aviation community and regional airlines. This system identifies traffic in a range of 35 to 40 NM of the aircraft, and issues traffic proximity (TA) warnings to help pilots in the visual acquisition of intruder aircraft. The TCAS I is mandatory for installation and use on aircraft with 10 to 30 seats.

The TCAS II system is a more sophisticated set. This system is internationally mandatory for aircraft with more than 30 seats, or weighing more than 15,000 kg (maximum takeoff weight). TCAS II provides TCAS I information, but also analyzes the projected flight path of the approaching aircraft. When the system detects the possibility of a collision or an imminent loss of separation, the TCAS II computer issues a Resolution Notice (RA). This is an auditory command for the pilot to take a specific evasive action. The computer is programmed in such a way that the pilot on the invading plane receives an AR for evasive action in the opposite direction (if it is equipped with TCAS II).

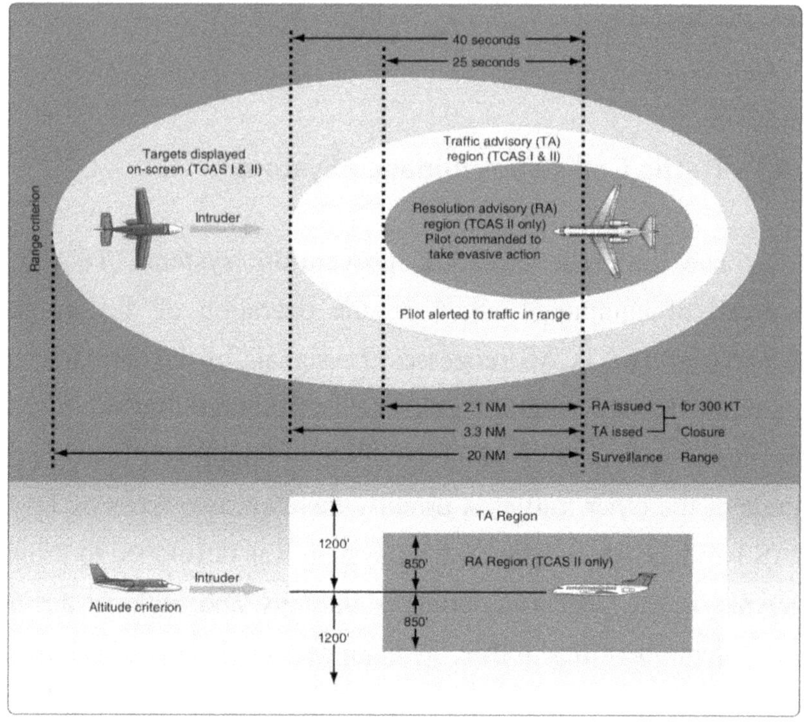

Extracto del documento sobre instrumentos de vuelo TCAS de FAA (federal aviation administration)

The transponder of an aircraft with TCAS can interrogate the transponders of other nearby aircraft using SSR (Mode C and Mode S) technology. This is achieved through the emission of a 1030 mHz signal. The transponders of interrogated aircraft respond with an encoded signal of 1090 mHz that allows the TCAS computer to show the position and altitude of each aircraft. If the aircraft is within the horizontal or vertical distances shown in the previous figure, an audible TA is announced. If this situation arises, the crew will have to decide if it is necessary to take action. Aircraft equipped with TCAS II use continuous response information, to analyze the speed and trajectory of the target aircraft in the vicinity. If it is estimated that a collision is imminent, an AR is emitted; where the system itself will indicate the evasive maneuver that is required to avoid the collision.

Aircraft equipped with different models of TCAS are displayed on a screen on the flight deck. Different colors and shapes are used to represent the approaching planes, depending on the level of imminent threat. Since ARs are currently limited to vertical evasive maneuvers, some independent TCAS displays are vertical electronic speed indicators. Most aircraft use some version of an electronic HSI on a screen or navigation page to display TCAS information.

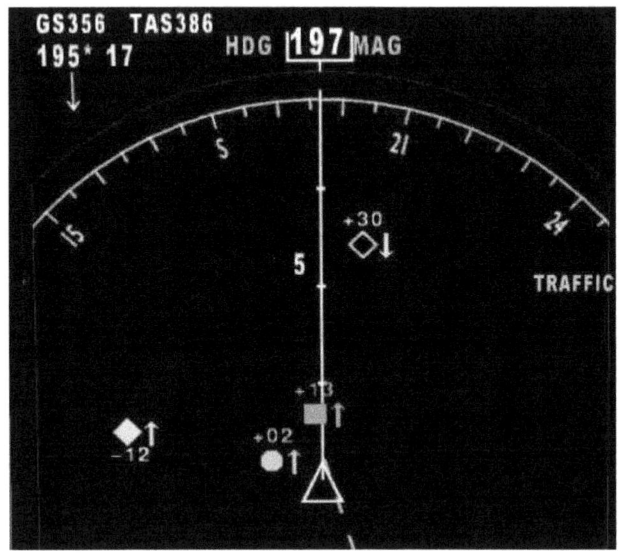

ELT - Emergency Locator Transmitter

The emergency locator beacon (ELT) is a device designed to locate the geographical position of an aircraft in the event of an accident or emergency landing at a remote point. The ELT is an emergency locator that has an independent battery-powered transmitter, which is activated in the presence of a peak of G-forces experienced during a crash. The activation of the ELT can also be done manually through a switch located in the cockpit, or from the same equipment installed on the aircraft. This equipment is mandatory in all aircraft, except for only a few specific cases, with local flight limitation, among others.

It is important to keep in mind that the ELT has a specific installation position on the aircraft. This is because the sensitivity and activation capacity of the G-Switch is given by the census of accelerations on the longitudinal axis of the equipment. That is, a value of extreme accelerations applied on another axis, may not activate the sensor and the equipment may not transmit despite the fact that the aircraft has had an impact with the terrain. In this regard, the equipment designed to be installed in helicopters must also be considered to have acceleration census systems different from those of fixed-wing aircraft. The helicopter, due to its particular flight mechanics and in the event of an accident, will present a breakdown of accelerations that are likely to be very different from that of

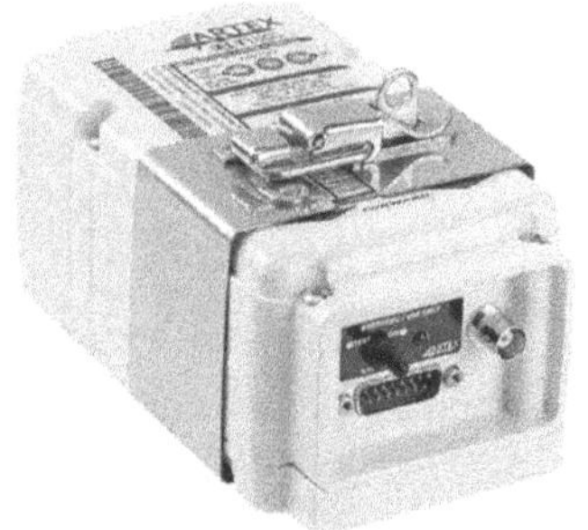

the aircraft. That is why ELTs for helicopters have differences in the census axes of accelerations.

The ELT transmits a digital signal every 50 seconds at a frequency of 406,025 MHz at 5 watts for at least 24 hours. The signal is received anywhere in the world by the satellites of the COSPAS-SARSAT international satellite system. Two types of satellites are used, low-Earth orbit (LEOSAT) and geostationary satellites (GEOSAT) with different complementary capabilities. The signal is partially processed and stored on satellites and then transmitted to ground stations known as local user terminals (LUT). The decryption of a signal is carried out in LUTs, and appropriate search and rescue operations are reported through the mission control centers (MCCs) established for this purpose.

For a better understanding of how it works, the specifications of one of the most widely used ELTs in general aviation worldwide are considered below: the Artex ELT 1000.

The Artex ELT 1000 emits in two bands at the same time: in 121.5 mHz (emission band of the first generation of ELT), and in frequency 406 mHz (current requirement for aeronautical certification). It has an autonomous emission capacity for 24 hours of pulses of 5W (440 m/s). To do this, it is equipped with lithium batteries (LiSO2) that have an average life of 6 years. Activation of the acceleration force sensor (G Switch) has a sensitivity of 2.3 G.

Although the ELT is a high-performance, certified and proven efficiency equipment, it has some "weaknesses" that sometimes make it impossible to activate in the event of an accident. The following are some of the variables that could condition the activation of the equipment or the lack of detection by the COSPAS-SARSAT system:

The emission antenna is installed in the fuselage of the aircraft (usually in the area of the tail structure, in light aircraft) and connected to the equipment through a cable. In an accident, both elements can be damaged and no matter how much the equipment is activated, it does not emit the signal.

If the impact mechanics do not have a peak deceleration in the longitudinal axis of the ELT, it is very likely that it will not be activated.

If the ELT is not properly registered and certified by the COSPAS-SARSAT service, it is likely that the signal received does not contain the precise information for the rescue.

The installation of the ELT in an inappropriate position on the aircraft can condition activation in the event of an accident.

The lack of replacement of the internal battery conditions the operation of the equipment.

The following image shows an unarmed Artex ELT; where it can be seen how the direction of installation of the equipment activation device ("G-Switch") is aligned with the indication of the direction of installation of all the equipment of the aircraft. The violent deceleration loads applied in that sense will be the ones that will activate the ELT.

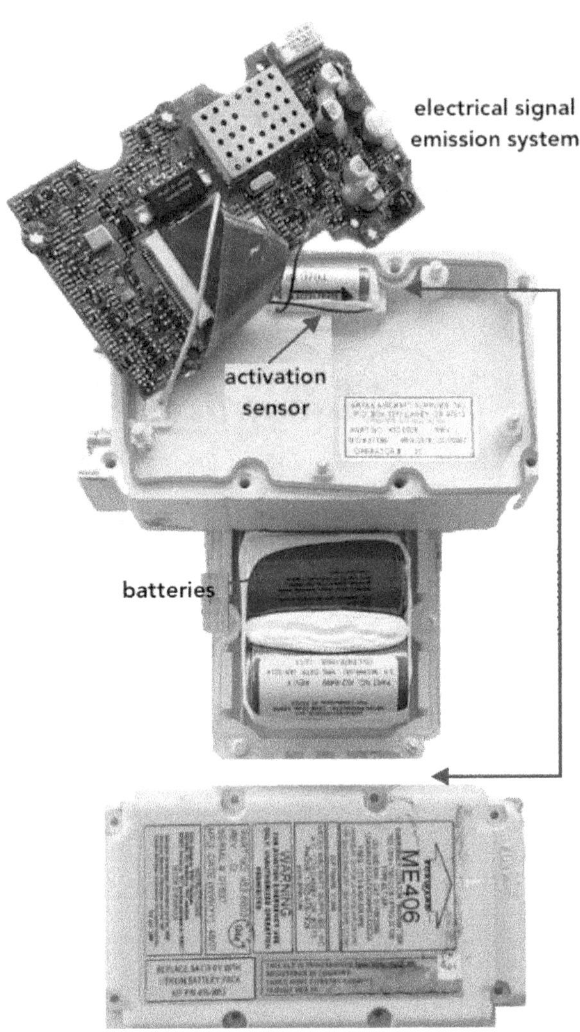

Biblioteca
Aeronáutica
aviación en simples pasos

Milton Keynes UK
Ingram Content Group UK Ltd.
UKHW021833041024
449101UK00012B/762